FEARFUL
JOURNEYS

Fife Council Education Department
King's Road Primary School
King's Crescent, Rosyth KY11 2RS

Compiled by
Wendy Body & Pat Edwards

Acknowledgements

We are grateful to the following for permission to reproduce copyright material: Edward Arnold (Publishers) Ltd for the story 'Oisin in the Land of Youth' from *Heroes and their Journeys* by Paul Groves and Nigel Grimshaw; John G Aylen, Ottawa, Canada, for the poem 'On the Way to the Mission' by Duncan Campbell Scott; Andre Deutsch Ltd for an extract from *Comfort Herself* by Geraldine Kaye; C J Fulcher on behalf of the author for the poem 'Night' by Richard McLaughlin from *First Year Poetry Anthology 1986-87*, compiled by C J Fulcher, produced by Chepstow Comprehensive School; Victor Gollancz Ltd for the chapter 'The Owl' from *Mrs Frisby and the Rats of Nimh* by Robert C O'Brien; Harper & Row, Inc for an extract from *The Deserter* by Nigel Gray. Copyright © 1977 Nigel Gray; the author and William Heinemann Ltd for an extract from *The Huntsman* by Douglas Hill (1982); Hodder & Stoughton Ltd for an extract from *The Incredible Journey* by Sheila Burnford. Copyright © 1960 by Sheila Burnford; Penguin Books Australia Ltd for an extract from *The Further Adventures of Dr A A A McGurk* by Osmar White, illustrated by Jeff Hook. Pages 32-7 were written by Peter Rooley and Bill Boyle. Pages 46-7 were written by Ron Stobbart.

We have been unable to trace the copyright holder in *Blind Flight* by Hilary Milton (pub Franklin Watts, Inc) and would appreciate any information that would enable us to do so.

We are grateful to the following for permission to reproduce photographs: B. & C. Alexander, pages 105, 106 *below right*, 110 *inset*; Allsport, pages 36 *centre* (photo Bernard Desestres), 36 *below left* (photo Steve Powell), 37 *above left inset* (photo Francois Rickard), 37 *below right inset* and 37 *background* (photos Simon Ward); Doug Allan, pages 109 *below*, 110/111 *background*; John Cleare/Mountain Camera, page 108 *below* (photo Colin Monteath); Colorsport, pages 36 *above right* (photo H Tavernier), 37 *below left*; Robert Harding Picture Library/Wally Herbert Collection, pages 104, 109 *above*; Heavylift Cargo Airlines Ltd, page 35; David Jamieson, page 36 *below right*; Geraldine Kaye, page 16; Adrian Meredith Photography, page 32 *inset*, 34; Oxford Scientific Films, pages 106 *above* (photo Leonard Lee Rue III), 106 *below left* (photo Doug Allan), 107 (photo Ben Osborne); Rolls-Royce plc, page 32/33; Scott Polar Research Institute, page 108 *above*; Sporting Pictures (UK), page 36 *above left*; Telegraph Colour Library, page 47 (photo R Barnes); J. Watkins, page 46.

Illustrators, other than those acknowledged with each story, include Jeannie Clark pp.16-17; Chris Evans pp.34-5; Judith L. Mitchell p.45; Allan Harris pp.46-7; Azoo pp.48-9; Jan van der Voo pp.78-81.

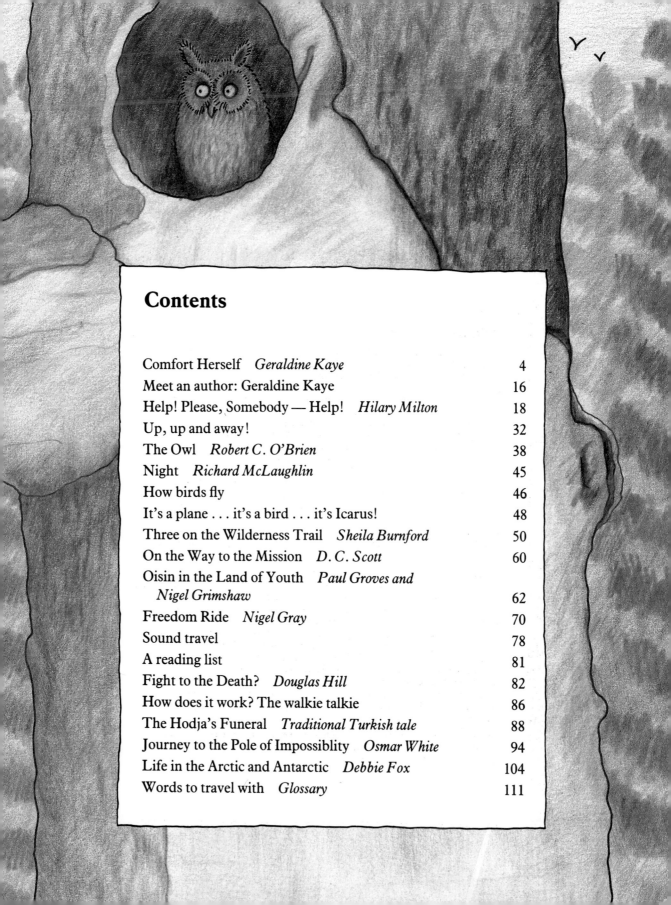

Contents

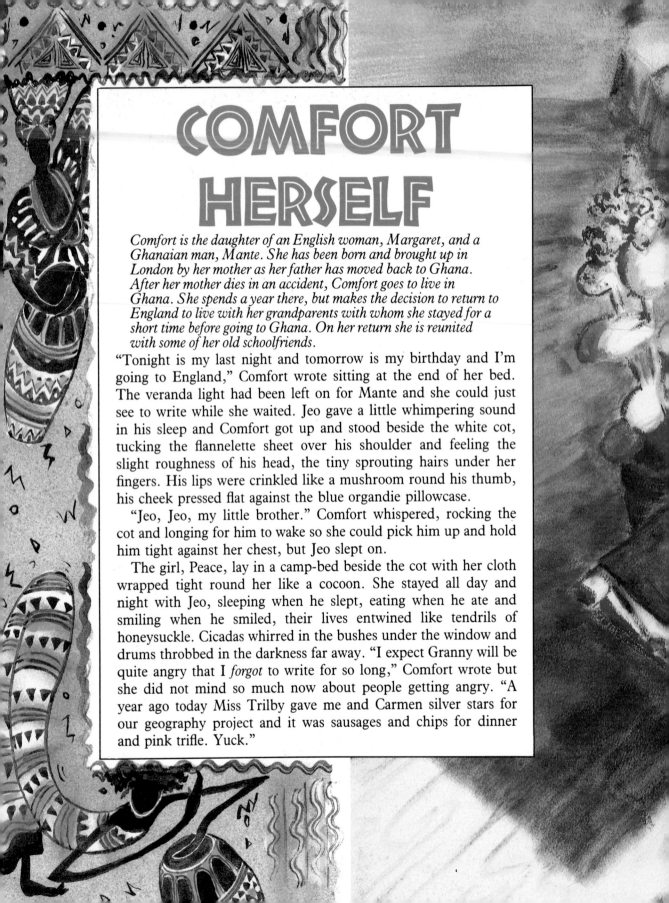

COMFORT HERSELF

Comfort is the daughter of an English woman, Margaret, and a Ghanaian man, Mante. She has been born and brought up in London by her mother as her father has moved back to Ghana. After her mother dies in an accident, Comfort goes to live in Ghana. She spends a year there, but makes the decision to return to England to live with her grandparents with whom she stayed for a short time before going to Ghana. On her return she is reunited with some of her old schoolfriends.

"Tonight is my last night and tomorrow is my birthday and I'm going to England," Comfort wrote sitting at the end of her bed. The veranda light had been left on for Mante and she could just see to write while she waited. Jeo gave a little whimpering sound in his sleep and Comfort got up and stood beside the white cot, tucking the flannelette sheet over his shoulder and feeling the slight roughness of his head, the tiny sprouting hairs under her fingers. His lips were crinkled like a mushroom round his thumb, his cheek pressed flat against the blue organdie pillowcase.

"Jeo, Jeo, my little brother." Comfort whispered, rocking the cot and longing for him to wake so she could pick him up and hold him tight against her chest, but Jeo slept on.

The girl, Peace, lay in a camp-bed beside the cot with her cloth wrapped tight round her like a cocoon. She stayed all day and night with Jeo, sleeping when he slept, eating when he ate and smiling when he smiled, their lives entwined like tendrils of honeysuckle. Cicadas whirred in the bushes under the window and drums throbbed in the darkness far away. "I expect Granny will be quite angry that I *forgot* to write for so long," Comfort wrote but she did not mind so much now about people getting angry. "A year ago today Miss Trilby gave me and Carmen silver stars for our geography project and it was sausages and chips for dinner and pink trifle. Yuck."

5

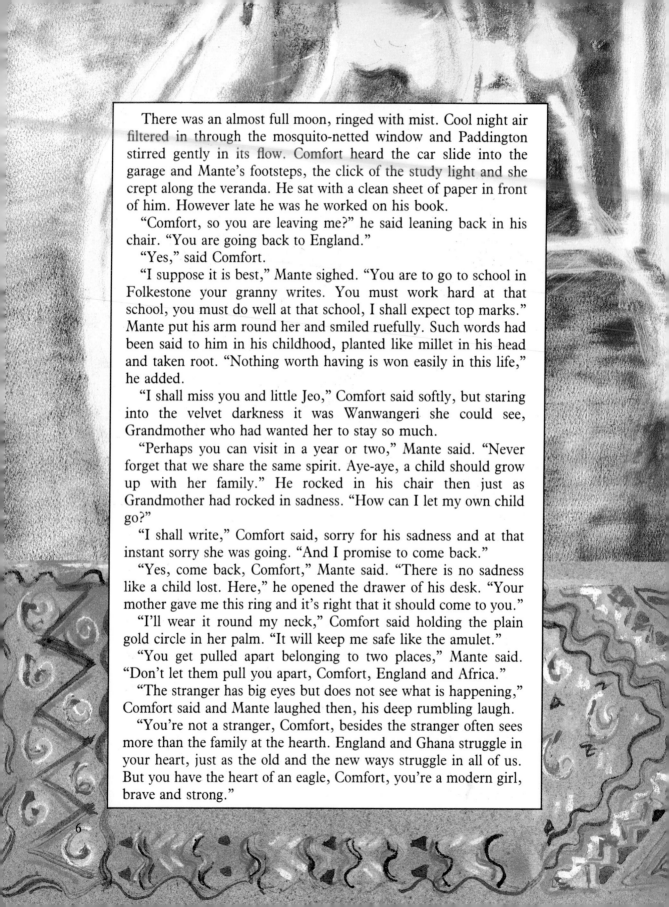

There was an almost full moon, ringed with mist. Cool night air filtered in through the mosquito-netted window and Paddington stirred gently in its flow. Comfort heard the car slide into the garage and Mante's footsteps, the click of the study light and she crept along the veranda. He sat with a clean sheet of paper in front of him. However late he was he worked on his book.

"Comfort, so you are leaving me?" he said leaning back in his chair. "You are going back to England."

"Yes," said Comfort.

"I suppose it is best," Mante sighed. "You are to go to school in Folkestone your granny writes. You must work hard at that school, you must do well at that school, I shall expect top marks." Mante put his arm round her and smiled ruefully. Such words had been said to him in his childhood, planted like millet in his head and taken root. "Nothing worth having is won easily in this life," he added.

"I shall miss you and little Jeo," Comfort said softly, but staring into the velvet darkness it was Wanwangeri she could see, Grandmother who had wanted her to stay so much.

"Perhaps you can visit in a year or two," Mante said. "Never forget that we share the same spirit. Aye-aye, a child should grow up with her family." He rocked in his chair then just as Grandmother had rocked in sadness. "How can I let my own child go?"

"I shall write," Comfort said, sorry for his sadness and at that instant sorry she was going. "And I promise to come back."

"Yes, come back, Comfort," Mante said. "There is no sadness like a child lost. Here," he opened the drawer of his desk. "Your mother gave me this ring and it's right that it should come to you."

"I'll wear it round my neck," Comfort said holding the plain gold circle in her palm. "It will keep me safe like the amulet."

"You get pulled apart belonging to two places," Mante said. "Don't let them pull you apart, Comfort, England and Africa."

"The stranger has big eyes but does not see what is happening," Comfort said and Mante laughed then, his deep rumbling laugh.

"You're not a stranger, Comfort, besides the stranger often sees more than the family at the hearth. England and Ghana struggle in your heart, just as the old and the new ways struggle in all of us. But you have the heart of an eagle, Comfort, you're a modern girl, brave and strong."

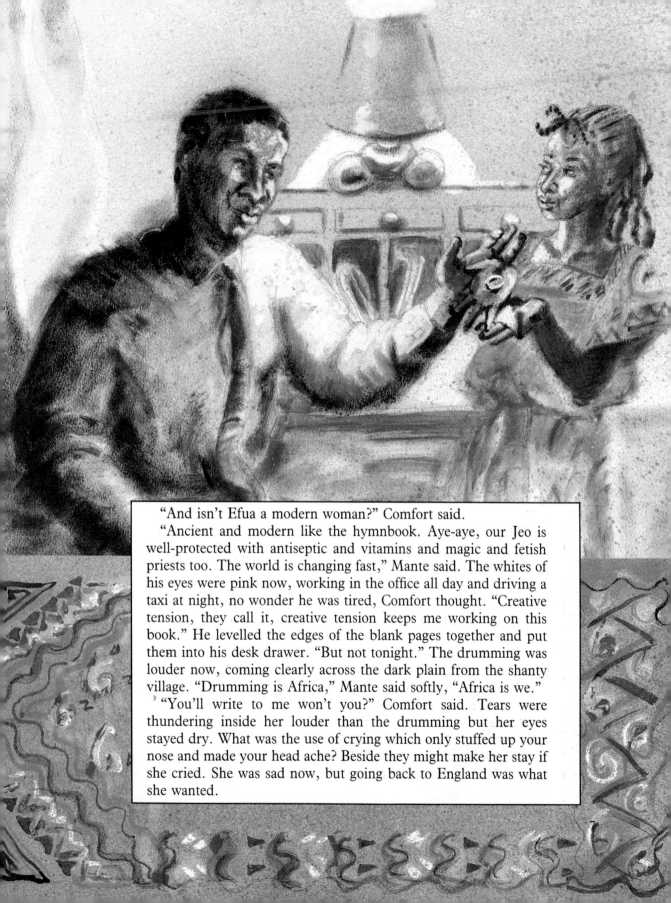

"And isn't Efua a modern woman?" Comfort said.

"Ancient and modern like the hymnbook. Aye-aye, our Jeo is well-protected with antiseptic and vitamins and magic and fetish priests too. The world is changing fast," Mante said. The whites of his eyes were pink now, working in the office all day and driving a taxi at night, no wonder he was tired, Comfort thought. "Creative tension, they call it, creative tension keeps me working on this book." He levelled the edges of the blank pages together and put them into his desk drawer. "But not tonight." The drumming was louder now, coming clearly across the dark plain from the shanty village. "Drumming is Africa," Mante said softly, "Africa is we."

"You'll write to me won't you?" Comfort said. Tears were thundering inside her louder than the drumming but her eyes stayed dry. What was the use of crying which only stuffed up your nose and made your head ache? Beside they might make her stay if she cried. She was sad now, but going back to England was what she wanted.

"Many happy returns, many happy returns, Comfort," Granny said hugging Comfort tight and just behind her Grandad polished the end of his nose with his hanky so it shone like a cherry.

"Can't call you little now, can we, twelve years old?"

"I should think not indeed," Granny said straightening her new cyclamen hat. "All your presents are at home ready."

"Presents?" said Comfort wonderingly, her head still full of engines roaring. "Home?"

"Back at Smithy Cottage," Granny said. "Bless me, the child has forgotten her birthday, whatever next?"

"It's my best day, the best day in the whole lot is June 12th," Grandad said.

"Forgetting your own birthday," Granny said fizzing like a sherbet stick with the excitement of it all. "You'll have to do better than that, Comfort. When I was your age lots of girls of twelve were earning their own living, straight into service, kitchen maids at twelve."

"I know," said Comfort catching Grandad's wink.

"And whatever are you wearing?" Granny said diving into the zip bag that Grandad was carrying. "Good job I brought your cardigan, I only hope it fits after all this time."

"It's nice and warm," Comfort said, pulling the dark green cardigan over her balloon-patterned cloth. "Thanks."

"Fits like a glove," Granny said triumphant. "You've changed Comfort, thinner altogether, and what ever have they done to your hair?"

"I like it like this," Comfort said patting the tiny braids that Ata had made in Wanwangeri. I shall keep it like this, I've washed it like this twice."

"Thank goodness for small mercies," Granny said.

In the train Granny talked and Comfort looked out at the greys and browns of London, back gardens with swings and sandpits and then the lush green of Kent. England was always the same but not quite the same. Would a blue sky always be as blue as Paddington's coat in Hillside Estate and would the rhythmic clank of the train always sound like the drumming in Wanwangeri, Comfort wondered, hugging the bundle on her knees.

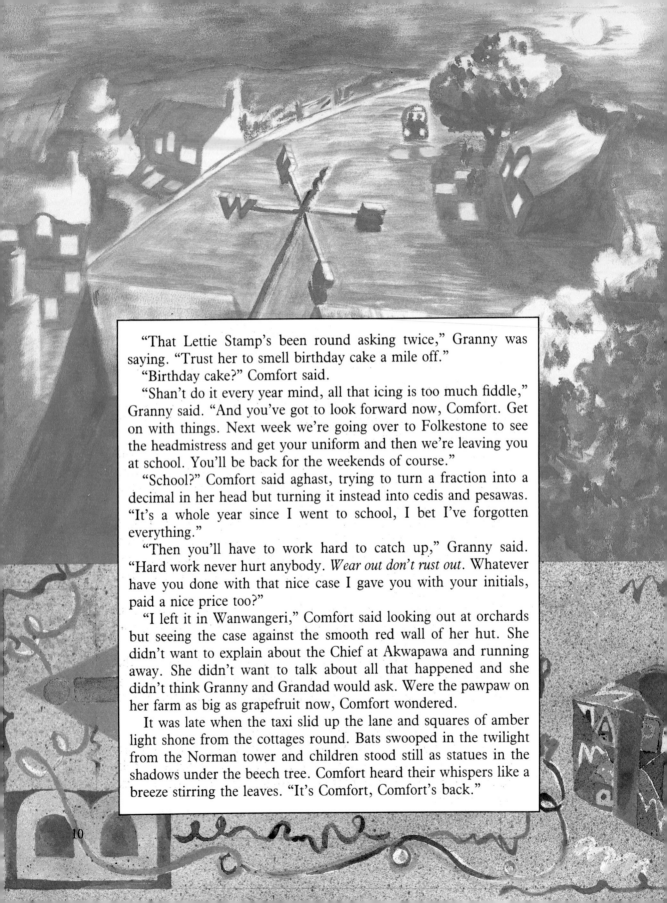

"That Lettie Stamp's been round asking twice," Granny was saying. "Trust her to smell birthday cake a mile off."

"Birthday cake?" Comfort said.

"Shan't do it every year mind, all that icing is too much fiddle," Granny said. "And you've got to look forward now, Comfort. Get on with things. Next week we're going over to Folkestone to see the headmistress and get your uniform and then we're leaving you at school. You'll be back for the weekends of course."

"School?" Comfort said aghast, trying to turn a fraction into a decimal in her head but turning it instead into cedis and pesawas. "It's a whole year since I went to school, I bet I've forgotten everything."

"Then you'll have to work hard to catch up," Granny said. "Hard work never hurt anybody. *Wear out don't rust out*. Whatever have you done with that nice case I gave you with your initials, paid a nice price too?"

"I left it in Wanwangeri," Comfort said looking out at orchards but seeing the case against the smooth red wall of her hut. She didn't want to explain about the Chief at Akwapawa and running away. She didn't want to talk about all that happened and she didn't think Granny and Grandad would ask. Were the pawpaw on her farm as big as grapefruit now, Comfort wondered.

It was late when the taxi slid up the lane and squares of amber light shone from the cottages round. Bats swooped in the twilight from the Norman tower and children stood still as statues in the shadows under the beech tree. Comfort heard their whispers like a breeze stirring the leaves. "It's Comfort, Comfort's back."

10

And then silence.

"I knew we should be tired," Granny said and if she heard the whispers too she gave no sign. "I left the table all laid ready, won't take a moment to heat up the soup."

"Can I open my presents now?" Comfort said. She unwrapped the crisp patterned paper, listening for the sounds outside. There was a small work-basket with needles and cottons and a blue letter-writing case fitted out with paper and envelopes.

"Practical presents," Granny said. "I always give practical presents. And what do you think of your birthday cake?" The cake on the dining room table was far from practical. A pale lilac cake with a tiny crinoline lady standing in the middle and the cake belling out round her.

"Oh, it's magic, gay as a pineapple," Comfort said and she flung her arms round Granny. "I never had such a fine-fine home-made birthday cake before."

"Tch, tch, it's nothing special, child," Granny said. "Just a light sponge mixture and two layers of butter icing. Oh, those silly children," she added as a shrill squeal came from the other side of the hedge.

"Can't they have some cake?" Comfort said.

"I didn't make this lovely cake for children screaming on the green," Granny said sharply. "Letting them play outside at this time of night. Take your presents upstairs, Comfort, while I just heat the soup."

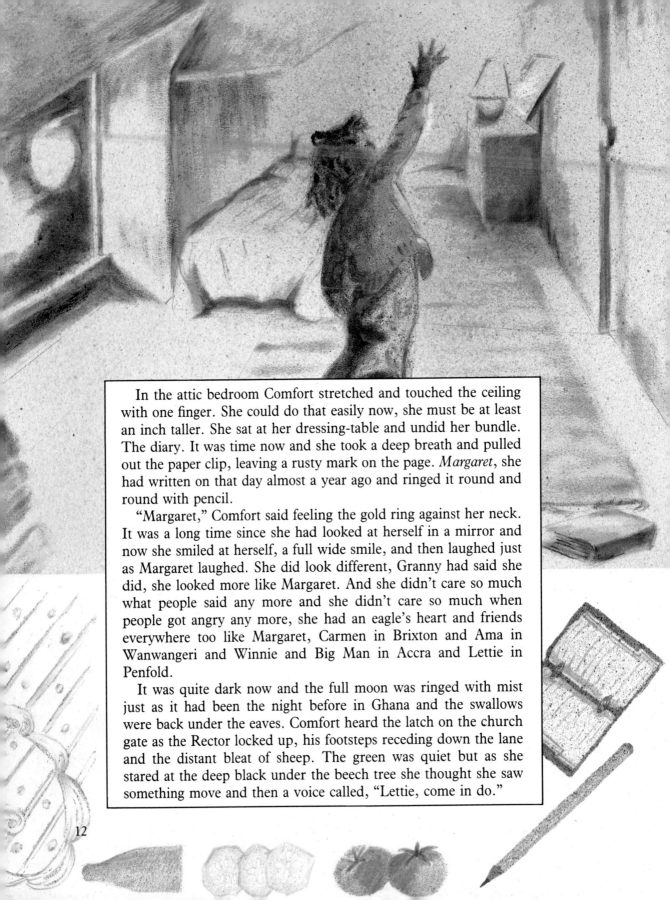

In the attic bedroom Comfort stretched and touched the ceiling with one finger. She could do that easily now, she must be at least an inch taller. She sat at her dressing-table and undid her bundle. The diary. It was time now and she took a deep breath and pulled out the paper clip, leaving a rusty mark on the page. *Margaret*, she had written on that day almost a year ago and ringed it round and round with pencil.

"Margaret," Comfort said feeling the gold ring against her neck. It was a long time since she had looked at herself in a mirror and now she smiled at herself, a full wide smile, and then laughed just as Margaret laughed. She did look different, Granny had said she did, she looked more like Margaret. And she didn't care so much what people said any more and she didn't care so much when people got angry any more, she had an eagle's heart and friends everywhere too like Margaret, Carmen in Brixton and Ama in Wanwangeri and Winnie and Big Man in Accra and Lettie in Penfold.

It was quite dark now and the full moon was ringed with mist just as it had been the night before in Ghana and the swallows were back under the eaves. Comfort heard the latch on the church gate as the Rector locked up, his footsteps receding down the lane and the distant bleat of sheep. The green was quiet but as she stared at the deep black under the beech tree she thought she saw something move and then a voice called, "Lettie, come in do."

"Lettie," Comfort whispered launching the words into the darkness like little boats. "Lettie where are you?"

But Granny was calling from downstairs. "Dinner's ready, Comfort."

"Shall I light the candles?" Comfort said carrying the cake to the deep window-sill in the thickness of the cottage wall. The match scratched on the box and the twelve candles on the crinoline skirt bloomed into little flames. Grandad put out the light.

"What a picture," Granny said spooning oxtail soup and smiling.

"Can I have the lady after?" Comfort said, thinking of the reindeer and sledge and a Christmas long ago.

"You'll have to take care of it, mind," Granny said. "It's real bone china."

"Corned beef and salad," Grandad said collecting up the plates. "And then cake for afters, seems a shame to cut it just for us?" The meal was almost finished when the gate flung back and footsteps scampered on the path and bubbles of giggle burst all round the dark garden.

"It's those children all over my garden, all over my roses," Granny said getting up. "Shoo, shoo."

"Only natural with Comfort back?" Grandad said. "They want to see our Comfort."

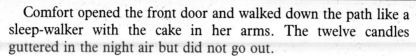

Comfort opened the front door and walked down the path like a sleep-walker with the cake in her arms. The twelve candles guttered in the night air but did not go out.

"You got back then," Lettie said, her eyes shining green as grapes in the candlelight. "Didn't know you were coming back, did I?"

"Neither did I." Comfort said. "Want some birthday cake?"

"You bet," said Lettie.

"Me too," said Colin and Betty and Ruth and Dave and Carol and Joy and little Freddie Bone. There were nine children in the garden now and more coming across the green in dressing-gowns as if the candles had called them back from sleep. They stood round the cake as Comfort set it on the grass. Even the Watkins children, smiling clumsily and pausing at the gate, half-expecting somebody might tell them to go away, but nobody did.

"You've got to blow this whole lot out, all the twelve in one blow," Lettie said, "then you can wish."

Comfort blew. A long blow that took all her breath, her face moving round the cake and round again like the sun round the earth, until the last candle winked and died. There was a smell of candlewax in the darkness. Grandad fetched a knife from the dining room and Granny switched on the porch light.

"That's a lovely little old cake that is," Lettie said with a quick glance at Granny as Comfort pressed the knife down. "Best cake, prettiest cake I ever did see."

"Just sponge and butter-icing," Comfort said surprising herself with Granny's voice. But it wasn't really surprising, she thought, as she cut the cake into slices, because she was partly made of Mante and Margaret and Grandmother in Wanwangeri and Granny in Penfold, and partly of everything that had happened to her, but the rest was unique, *Comfort herself*.

"What did you want to come back here for?" Colin said with his hair falling over his eyes and his mouth full of cake.

"Stop asking silly questions," Lettie said. "This is where she belongs isn't it? Comfort Kwatey-Jones lives in Penfold, Kent, England, the World."

Written by Geraldine Kaye
Illustrated by Jeannie Clark

Meet an Author

GERALDINE KAYE

Geraldine Kaye was born and educated in England, but has since spent many years abroad, teaching in Singapore and Ghana. At the moment she lives in England, but her secret wish is to go back to Africa again.

Geraldine Kaye's favourite subject at school was English. She didn't like hockey, lacrosse or having to swim in the cold, grey sea! She loved chocolate eclairs. (Now she prefers prawns!) Her best-loved stories were Black Beauty and Little Women. Nowadays her favourite kind of book is one written by or about an unusual and original woman. Geraldine enjoys swimming, walking and visits to the theatre. She hates sore throats, being in a hurry, having bills to pay and her car breaking down!

Geraldine Kaye describes how she became a writer:

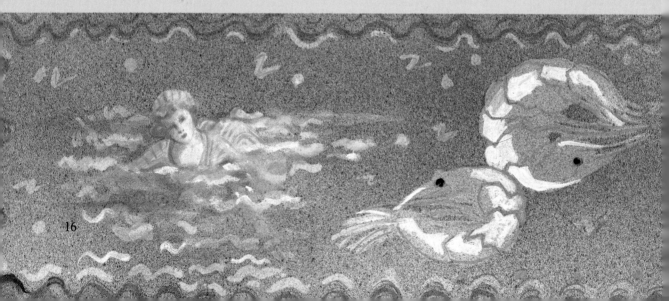

My great grandfather was a writer and I wanted to be one from an early age. From ten to fourteen I spent most of my homework time writing stories but then I had to stop because school work got more difficult. In my twenties I was teaching at a school in Singapore where all the girls and teachers were Asian. I wrote my first book 'Kassim Goes Fishing' about a Malay boy. Later I lived in Ghana and wrote several books with an African background. I also met the orphaned girl on whom 'Comfort Herself' is based and determined to write the story. However when I returned to England I became very interested in gypsies and wrote 'Nowhere to Stop' and 'A Different Sort of Christmas' about them and then as my own children grew up I wrote teenage books such as 'Runaway Boy', 'Joey's Room' and 'Marie Alone.' In recent years I have started thinking about Africa again and have written 'Comfort Herself' at last and now a sequel 'Great Comfort' which was published in Autumn 1988.

HELP! PLEASE, SOMEBODY–HELP!

Debbie is desperate. She's 3000 feet above sea level in a small plane. Her Uncle Walt, the pilot, is unconscious. A wild goose smashed through the windscreen. It hit him full in the chest and he cracked his head on the wheel as he fell over. The raw wind roars through the shattered windscreen. It's freezing cold. Although her uncle had taught her a little bit about flying, she has never flown alone. And she's blind!

Debbie shuddered. She gasped for breath but felt the force of the wind take it from her. She cupped her right hand over her nose, shielding the wind's harshness, and breathed once more. She fought to keep back the sobs, fought to clear her mind of the grip of panic.

She clenched her teeth and made herself relax her hold on the wheel.

Debbie couldn't see Uncle Walt's face but she knew he was unconscious. Three thousand feet above the ground. Nobody knew where they were, nobody could come looking for them, nobody could even hear her. Once more she took a deep breath, this time forcing out the rush of freezing wind. Holding onto the wheel with her right hand, she caught the headset wire and followed it down to the instrument panel. There, her fingers fumbled right and left, searching for the knob. Had to be a knob, had to be some way to turn the radio control, had to be some way to call for help.

Finally, she found a knob and for a moment thought she should take off her glove. But the wind was blowing too hard and she knew that if she took it off and dropped it, she'd never find it again.

Carefully holding the wheel, neither pulling nor pushing, she felt the dial, tested it, and found that it would move. She cautiously turned it clockwise until it could go no further, then she gradually turned it back in the opposite direction. After each move of what she supposed was less than a quarter of an inch, she paused, swallowed, and said aloud, "Help me! Please, somebody, help me!"

But each time she was greeted with nothing except static, static, static.

Once, when she had the knob turned almost as far to the left as it would go, she thought she heard a voice. Jerking her hand away so she wouldn't accidentally lose the spot on the dial, she called once more. This time she repeated a word she'd heard before. "Please, somebody — mayday! *Mayday!*"

But the fuzzy voice she heard did not stop, did not interrupt itself for her cry.

Debbie shuddered all over. Alone. Blind. Flying over somewhere, she didn't know where, not knowing what was wrong with Uncle Walt or who to call or how to fly the plane —

North!

Uncle Walt had said they were heading north toward Red Mountain and Birmingham. But she didn't want to go that way. She wanted to go back to the farm, back to her mother and Aunt Eva and Rick.

She sniffed and tried to remember how Uncle Walt had turned the plane. The wheel, she knew about the wheel, but she'd also felt some kind of pressure on one of the pedals. The left — no, no, the right.

That was it. He had pushed down on the right pedal and turned the wheel to the right. And, wait now, something else.

She shook her head, what, what?

Her arms — something should happen to her arms. The elbows seemed to have bent when he turned. And the wheel came back a little. Just a little.

She couldn't do it but she had to do it. She had to try.

Holding her breath, putting her right foot firmly on the pedal, she slowly turned the wheel, holding back, but not too much.

Nothing — no, wait — it was turning. The plane was slowly turning to the right.

What had she counted? Eight? Five? Nine? She couldn't remember but she thought it was seven.

One, two — too fast — three, four, five — wait, it was four. That was the count before. Without stopping to think, she eased the wheel back and turned it the other way until it was set with her hands straight across from one another. She let off the right pedal and pressed the left one lightly.

When she sensed that the Kadet was flying straight and level once more, she thought about the way the sun was coming into the cockpit. She couldn't be positive, but it seemed to be coming at a different angle.

She swallowed, counted to ten, and once more made the same kind of turn. This time, when she brought it level again, she tried to tell herself that she was heading back toward home. But she knew that even if she flew right over the farm, even if by some miracle she could get the Kadet right over the runway, she wouldn't know it. And could not land it.

She choked back a sob and once more reached for the radio. She followed the same procedure she'd used earlier — turn it a fraction of an inch, stop, call for help, listen, turn again and call again and listen again.

Once, when the static seemed louder than before, she was certain that she'd located a ground station or even another aircraft. She called for help, she yelled "Mayday!" until her voice was raw, her lungs burning. Nothing.

She had no idea where the dial was set or how many times she had screamed into the microphone when suddenly she found a clear spot on the dial. She listened. There were no voices but something was different, something was special about this one spot. She took a deep breath and held it until she could not hold it any longer. Then, at the top of her voice, she called out, "Help me! Somebody — anybody — please help me. Mayday, mayday, *mayday!*"

Then she waited . . .

Charter Flight 640, bound for Kansas City on its return leg from Orlando, Florida, was cruising easily at thirty thousand feet. Jeffrey Billings, the pilot, eased back into his seat, turned his headset mike to the side, and reached for his plastic cup. He took a quick sip, then turned toward Steve Lincoln, his co-pilot. "Going to the game tomorrow?"

"The Chiefs?"

"Sure the Chiefs — who else?"

"I thought they were on the road tomorrow."

"Tomorrow it's the Raiders and Chiefs."

"Hey, that's supposed to be next week —"

"It's tomorrow."

"Are you sure?" Steve pushed aside his own mike. "I've got tickets to that game but I thought it was a week off. And I promised Virginia I'd take her down to the farm." He made a face. "I think she conned me."

"It happens," Jeff said. "Anyway, if you've got tickets and can't make it, I'll take them off your hands. Nan's brother and his fiancée are in town —"

"*Help me, please — somebody help me!*"

The suddenness of the sound made both men stop talking. Steve's eyebrows went up and he sat forward. Instinctively, Jeff slapped his mike into position.

"Please — if anybody hears me, please help. Mayday, mayday, *mayday!*"

Jeff touched his headset. "This is Charter Flight 640. I hear you. What's the nature of your emergency?"

For a moment there was silence, then the voice came back. "Huh? I mean — it's me, I mean — are you talking to me?"

21

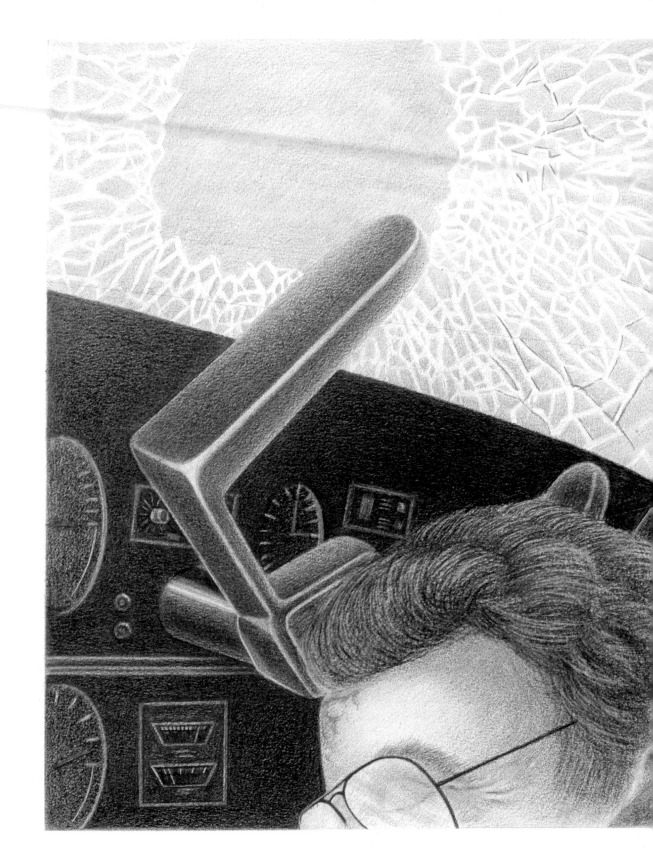

Jeff glanced at Steve and frowned. He cupped his hand over the mike. "Did you hear what I heard? Sounds like somebody's not sure what's going on." He moved his hand. "I say again, this is Charter Flight 640. If you're in trouble, perhaps I can help."

They heard a cough, then a quick, choking sob. "Mister, you've got to help me because I'm all by myself — I mean, I'm not by myself, I don't know what's wrong with my uncle — you have to do something. Please —"

The sound broke off once more and again Jeff glanced at Steve. "Whoever it is, she's not making herself clear."

"Sounds scared."

"Sure sounds something." Jeff took a deep breath. "Now — whoever you are, calm down. Try to think clearly. We'll help if we can, but you'll have to tell me what's wrong."

Once more, they heard a soft sob, then a voice said, "I — I'll try, mister, but I need help. Lots of it. I'm in a little plane and the pilot is my uncle and he's unconscious and I can't fly." Another sob. "Help me."

Steve turned quickly about. "It's a kid."

Jeff's experienced eye swept the instrument panel, catching his airspeed, his altitude, and the radio frequency, "Are you losing altitude — are you going down?"

"I — I don't think so. But I can't fly and my uncle won't answer me."

"All right, all right," Jeff said, keeping his voice slow and easy. "Now listen to me. First, what's your name?"

"Debbie — Debbie Whitfield."

"All right, Debbie. My name's Jeff. How old are you?"

"Thirteen."

"Do you know anything at all about flying? *Anything?*"

"I've been up here with my uncle before. He lets me hold the wheel, maybe put my feet on the pedals."

"Do you know what those controls do?"

"Not much but some. They make the plane turn and if I pull the wheel back, it goes up some."

"Good." Jeff turned to Steve. "Quick — what's the emergency frequency for Birmingham?"

Steve picked up a plastic-coated card and ran his finger down the printed lines. "Looks like it's one-twenty-one-point-five."

Jeff nodded and turned his attention back to his mike. "Debbie, is your plane going up or down?"

"Neither one, I think. But the windshield is broken out and the wind is freezing me."

"Good Lord," Steve said softly. "That child is in trouble."

Jeff nodded but kept his voice low and soft. "Do you know what happened — why your uncle is unconscious?"

"A wild goose or duck crashed through the windshield — that's all I know. But I'm cold and scared and I need lots of help. Lots of it."

"We'll help you," Jeff said.

"How?" Steve asked, studying the card once more. "All we can do is hope and pray the thing glides to a clear field before it crashes."

"Debbie, what kind of aircraft is it?"

"I think it's a Kadet."

Steve frowned, seemed to think for a moment, then said, "Hey, ask her what field she took off from".

Jeff relayed the query.

"No field. Not a real airport, I mean. My uncle has his own runway."

Steve's frown disappeared. "I know the craft — they call it a Tahoe Kadet. A lot like a Piper Vagabond except it doesn't require much runway." He tapped the card. "That's a plus — they say those things are pretty good gliders."

"Please — hurry!"

"We're going to help," Jeff said. "Now listen to me carefully, Debbie." He paused. "Are your hands on the wheel?"

"Yes."

"And your feet can reach the pedals?"

"Yes."

"All right. Now hold a little back pressure — do you know what I mean?"

"I — I think so."

"Make sure you don't pull the wheel toward you — but don't let it go forward. And keep even pressure on the pedals."

"All right — but it's cold and my face is freezing —"

"And you're a brave young girl," Jeff said quickly. "Just hold on. I'm going to switch my radio and call for somebody to help you —"

"*Don't leave me! Please!*"

"I'm not leaving you. I'm just going to call for more help. But whatever you do, don't touch your radio dial."

"All right. But hurry. Please hurry!"

"I'm hurrying," Jeff said. He reached for the knob but before turning it he read the frequency counter very carefully. "One-one-seven-point-nine," he said aloud.

"Got it," Steve said quickly.

Deftly, then, he turned the knob, stopping precisely on 121.5.

"Birmingham Control, Birmingham Control, this is Charter Flight six-four-zero — do you copy?"

Immediately a clear female voice came back to him. "I copy, six-four-zero."

"We just received a mayday call. Repeat — we just received a mayday call."

"I understand, six-four-zero. Do you know the nature of the emergency?"

"Affirmative," and Jeff repeated what Debbie had told him.

"What is the location?"

"I'm not certain, but right now we're ten minutes south-south-east of your city. The young girl's name is Debbie and she's monitoring frequency one-one-seven-point-nine. That's one-one-seven-point-nine."

"I understand, Captain — ?"

"The name's Billings, Jeff Billings. And you're — ?"

"Mindy — Mindy Jowers." There was a brief pause. "I'm switching to her frequency now."

"I'll tag along," Jeff said. Leaning forward, he carefully tuned the dial to 117.9. "Debbie?"

"I'm here. Did you get anybody?"

"I did." He paused.

"Debbie?"

"Yes — yes, ma'am?"

"This is Birmingham Control — just call me Mindy. Captain Billings told me what you're doing — "

"I'm not doing anything — just freezing and I need somebody to help. Real bad."

"We'll help," Mindy said simply. "You said you took off from your uncle's farm. Where is it?"

"Not far from Redfern — about five miles, I think. But I don't know where it is now — "

"I know," Mindy said calmly. "But think now — when your uncle took off, did he fly east or west?"

"I — I'm not sure. But maybe west."

"Toward the Tri-County Airport?"

"He didn't say."

"If you went west from Redfern, that would be toward Tri-County." Once more she paused. "How long had you been flying when the accident happened?"

"I'm not sure. Maybe fifteen minutes. Maybe twenty."

"But not long?"

"No. But somebody's got to do something because I can't fly and I don't know what to do and we'll crash and I'm — "

"Debbie!"

The sternness of Mindy's voice surprised Jeff and he was about to tell her to take it easy when he realised what she was doing.

"Yes, ma'am." Debbie's voice was still at the edge of panic. "But I've got to tell you — "

"Give me your uncle's name," Mindy interrupted.

"Walter Hodges — "

"All right. Now — Captain Billings?"

"Yes?"

"Can you tell Debbie what to do with her plane for a few minutes while — "

"But I can't do anything!" And now the shrillness in her voice could not be denied. "I can't even see! I'm *blind*!"

Jeff swallowed hard, turned and stared at Steve. "I don't believe it. Did you hear what she said?"

"I heard," Steve said, shaking his head. "Man, can you imagine what it's like. I've flown blind trainers before. But a kid? — What can we do?"

"Debbie, Debbie," and Mindy's words came soft and easy — it was as if Debbie had said no more than 'I'm cold' — "we'll get you down safely. Believe it."

Steve turned suddenly to Jeff. "Am I hearing what I think I'm hearing? How? How does she think anybody can talk that kid down — "

Jeff put his fingers to his lips. "Shhh. Don't want her to overhear you."

"And I'm scareder than I've ever been."

"I know," Mindy kept her words coming even and reassuring. "Would you believe I am, too?"

"What've you got to be afraid of?" The shrillness had slowly left Debbie's voice, and now her words came clear, though still strained. "You're on the ground and safe."

"I'm afraid you won't like me because I yelled at you just now, and because I can't come up and land the plane for you."

"But you would if you could."

"That I would. Now, believe me — we'll get you down safely."

"But hurry."

"We will," Mindy said. She paused a moment, then said, "Captain Billings will give you some instructions while I call the Civil Air Patrol and the Tri-County Airport."

Jeff gave Steve a swift glance, then concentrated on the radio microphone. He'd done some instructing shortly before leaving the Air Force. But teaching cadets was one thing. Telling a young blind girl in a disabled aircraft how to stay aloft was something entirely different. He took a deep breath, remembering how little time he had left before flying out of probable range.

"Debbie, listen very carefully. Pretend I'm your uncle, sitting right there beside you. I'm going to tell you how to stay up and fly over the same general area until Miss Jowers gets her people busy. Okay?"

"Okay — but if they don't hurry — it's too cold up here and my hands are getting numb and my face hurts."

"You can do it," Jeff said softly. "I know you can. Listen carefully." He stopped, took a deep breath, and continued. "Keep both hands on the wheel, with just enough back pressure to keep the nose up. Got it?"

"Yes, sir."

"Hey, how about 'Roger'?"

"All right — Roger."

"And keep both feet on the pedals."

"Ro — Roger."

"Now — turn the wheel slightly to the right — a little more back pressure, a little downward push on the right pedal — got that?"

"Roger."

"Now — count to six with me — one — two — three — four — five — six. Now, a little push on the left pedal and a little turn of the wheel to the left. One — two. Now — tell me how you feel — straight up or leaning?"

"I — I think I'm straight up."

"Good girl. I bet you'd make a real pilot. Sure would like to teach you. Now, count ten — yes, I'll count with you."

When they reached ten, he told her to repeat the steps for the turn they'd just executed. And when she'd levelled off and told him she thought she was sitting even again, he nodded. "Now, Miss Jowers'll be on the radio in a few seconds.

What you're doing is flying over the same area — makes it easier for other pilots to find you. And you won't stray too far. Okay?"

"I — Roger."

"You know, if I didn't have all these people with me, I'd stay right up here and help. Even with this jet. But — "

"I'm back, Captain."

"There she is now, Debbie. You're going to be all right — count on it. You call me on the phone tonight and tell me how it came out — will you?"

"I — I guess so."

"Oh, one last thing. I think you said earlier that you were about three thousand feet up — "

"Uncle Walt said thirty-six hundred feet above sea level, whatever that means."

"Means if the ocean were right below you, you'd be thirty-six hundred feet above it. That's a good altitude. You want to keep it — no higher or lower — "

"She can't read the altimeter or the airspeed indicator," Steve whispered urgently.

Jeff nodded. "You'll have to fly by the seat of your pants."

"Huh?"

"That's an old flying expression — something pilots used to do when their instruments didn't work. You sit perfectly still after each turn, relax as much as you can, and *feel* your position. You know — does it feel like you're leaning forward or backward. If you think you're leaning forward, pull the wheel back just a little. If you think you're leaning back, just push the wheel away from you. But easy — real easy."

"I'll try."

"You'll *do* it — okay?"

"I — Roger."

"And don't forget — you're to call me tonight. I'll let somebody know how to get in touch."

"I'll try. And, Captain — Jeff?"

"What is it, sweetheart?"

"Thank you."

Jeff rubbed the back of his hand across his face and took a deep breath. "Talk to you later."

Written by Hilary Milton
Illustrated by Maria Parrott.

UP, UP & *AWAY!*

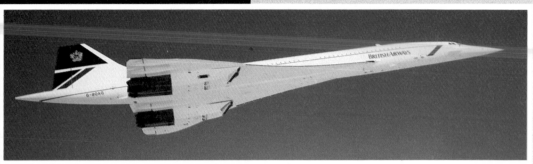

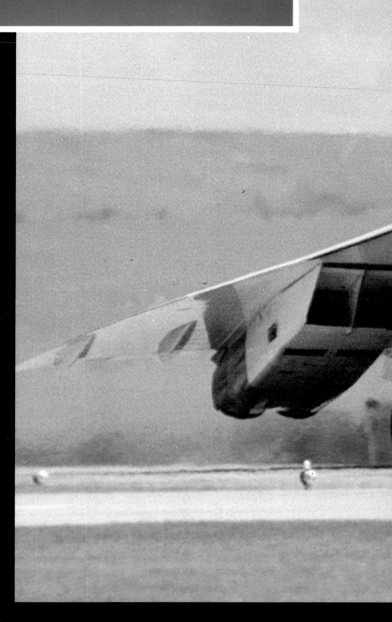

For centuries men watched the birds flying and longed to be able to do the same. They built all kinds of weird and wonderful 'flying' machines but it was only in 1903 that the Wright brothers made the first powered flight at Kittyhawk, North Carolina. Since then all kinds of aircraft have been developed and men have travelled to the moon and back in the Apollo space capsules.

Concorde is the fastest airliner in the world. It was designed and built by British and French aircraft companies and is a supersonic plane — in fact, it can travel at more than twice the speed of sound, or around 1,450 miles per hour. It has been in service with British Airways and Air France since 1976 and can carry 128 passengers from London to New York in just over three hours. It is possible to have breakfast before your flight leaves London and to reach New York in time for another breakfast, because of the time difference between Europe and the United States!

Shaped like a dart, Concorde slips easily through the air to reach its high speeds. The long pointed nose can be tilted downwards to help the pilots get a clearer view of the runway on take-off and landing. In the end only twenty Concordes were built but there are more than 110 miles of wiring in each aircraft!

MODERN PASSENGER AIRCRAFT

There are many types of airliner that can carry people to all parts of the world, either on holiday or on business trips. Such flights may be domestic or international, shorthaul or longhaul, scheduled or charter. There are also luxury executive jets, fitted out with bathrooms and comfortable lounges.

The illustration shows how up to 500 passengers and 20 crew members can be fitted into a modern 'jumbo' jet, such as the Boeing 747.

economy-class cabin

galley

upper deck

circular staircase between decks

flight deck

toilet

first-class cabin (typically 32 seats)

Typical flight deck of a modern passenger jet airline.

galley area

rear cabin

toilets

AIR CARGO

Planes carry freight as well as people — in fact most long distance, scheduled flights now carry both at the same time. However, there are some cargo-only planes, known as freighters, and some of these carry the most unusual things ... animals, fresh fruit and flowers, cars and trucks, helicopters and boats! Computers can be used to plan how to load such awkward cargoes — like the truck shown in the illustration

UP, UP & AWAY!

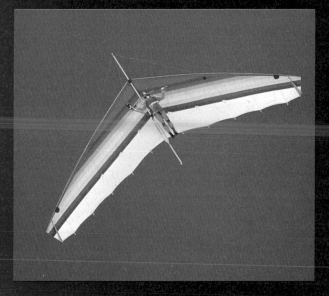
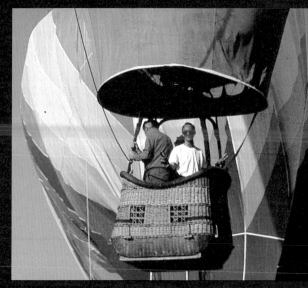

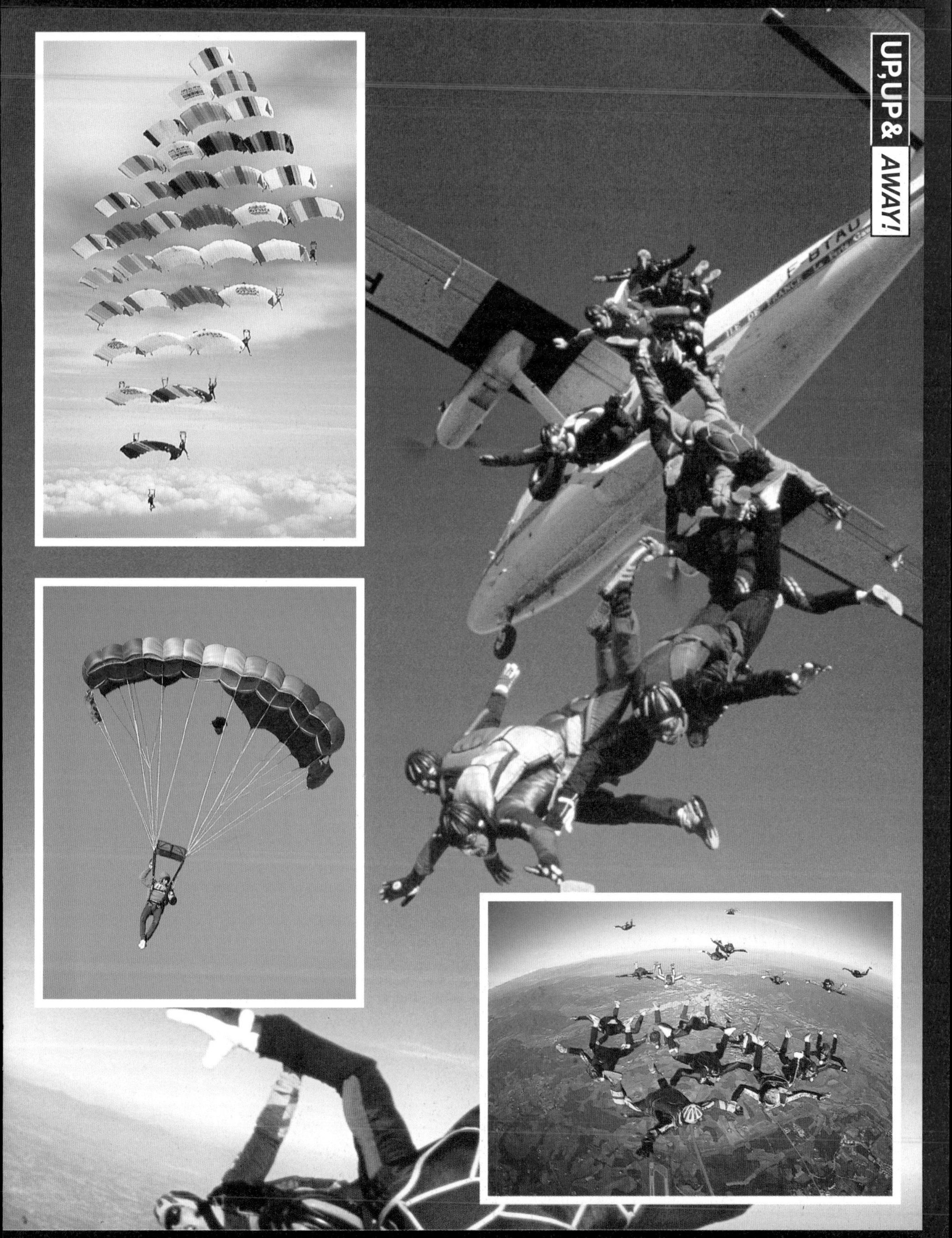
F-BTAU

The Owl

Mrs Frisby, the fieldmouse,
must move her family before the
farmer ploughs the field in which they live.
But her youngest son, Timothy, is very ill and cannot travel.
She does not know how to solve her problem,
so Jeremy, a friendly crow, promises to take her
to see someone who may help.

JEREMY APPEARED as promised when the last thumbnail of sun winked out over the mountains beyond the meadow. Mrs Frisby was waiting, her heart pounding in her ears, and three of the children were there to watch — Teresa and Martin standing beside their mother, and Cynthia, who was afraid of the crow, just a pair of round eyes peering out of the round doorway. Timothy was down below, taking a nap, and had not been told about the expedition lest he worry and blame himself for the risk his mother must take. (Indeed, the words Moving Day had not been mentioned in his presence.) Even to the other children Mrs Frisby had explained only a part of the problem; that is, she had not told them that there were only five days left, nor anything about Mr Fitzgibbon and the tractor. She did not want to worry them, either.

Jeremy landed with a *swoosh* — a bit dramatically, perhaps —
and nodded at the children and Mrs Frisby.

"Hello," he said. "Here I am."

Mrs Frisby introduced Martin and Teresa (and Cynthia's
eyes). Martin, who wished he were going on the trip himself,
asked Jeremy in excitement:

"How high can you fly?"

"Oh, I don't know exactly," Jeremy said. "A couple of miles,
I suppose."

"Mother, did you hear? You'll be two *miles* up in the air."

"Martin, it won't be necessary to go so high on this trip."

Jeremy said cheerfully: "No, but I can, if you'd like."

"No, thank you. I wouldn't think of your taking the
trouble." She was trying hard to hide her terror, and Martin had
not helped matters at all. But Jeremy suddenly saw that she was
trembling and realized that she must be afraid.

"It's all right," he said kindly. "There's nothing to be nervous
about. I fly over the woods a dozen times a day."

Yes, thought Mrs Frisby, but *you're* not riding on your back,
and *you* can't fall off.

"All right," she said as bravely as she could. "I'm ready.
Teresa and Martin, take care of Timothy until I come back, and
be sure you don't tell him where I've gone." With a small leap
she was on Jeremy's back, lying as flat as she could and holding
tight to the glossy feathers between his wings, as a horseback
rider grips the horse's mane before a jump. Martin and Teresa
waved goodbye, but she did not see them, for she had her face
pressed against the feathers and her eyes closed.

Once again she felt the surge of power as the crow's broad wings beat down against the air; this time it lasted longer for they were going higher than before. Then the beating became gentler as they levelled off, and then, to her alarm, it stopped altogether. What was wrong? The crow must have felt her grow tense, for suddenly from ahead she heard his voice:

"An updraft," he said. "We're soaring. There's usually one over this stretch of woods in the evening." A current of warm air, rising from the woods, was carrying them along. So smooth was the motion that they seemed to stand still, and Mrs Frisby ventured to open her eyes and lift her head just a trifle. She could not look straight down — that was Jeremy's back — but off to the right, and a bit behind them, she saw a grey-brown square the size of a postage stamp. She realized with a gasp that it was the garden patch, and Martin and Teresa, if they were still there, were too small to be seen.

"Look to the left," said Jeremy, who was watching her over his shoulder. She did, and saw what looked like a wide, fearsome snake, blue-green in colour, coiling through the woods.

"What is it?" she asked in wonder.

"You really don't know? It's the river."

"Oh," said Mrs Frisby, rather ashamed of her ignorance. She had heard of the river, of course, but had not known that it looked like a snake. She had never been there, since to reach it one had to cross the entire width of the forest. There were advantages to being a bird.

In a minute more they had left the updraft, and Jeremy's
wings resumed pumping. They went higher, and Mrs Frisby
closed her eyes again. When she opened them, the garden patch
had vanished far behind them, and Jeremy, searching the trees
below, began a long slanting descent. Eventually, as he banked
sharply, Mrs Frisby saw off his wing tip a grey-brown patch
among a group of tall green pines; from so high it looked like a
gnarled grey bush, but as they circled lower she could see that it
was in fact an enormous tree, leafless, skeletal, and partly dead.
One huge branch had recently broken off and fallen, and three
pine trunks lay bent double under its weight. It was a gloomy
and primeval spot, deeply shadowed in the grey dusk. Jeremy
circled over it one more time, looking at a certain mark
three-fourths of the way up the towering main trunk. Just
below this spot another great branch, itself as big as an ordinary
tree, jutted out over the tops of the pines, and on this at last
Jeremy fluttered gently to rest. They were some ten feet from
the main trunk, and Mrs Frisby could see, just above the place
where the branch joined the tree, a dark round hole as large as a
lunch plate.

"We're here," Jeremy said in a low voice. "There's where he
lives."

"Should I get down?" Instinctively, Mrs Frisby spoke in a
whisper.

"Yes. We've got to walk closer. But quietly. He doesn't like
loud noises."

"It's so high." She still clung to the crow's back.

"But the limb is broad. You'll be safe enough."

And indeed the limb was almost as wide as a pavement. Mrs Frisby gathered her courage, slithered down, and felt the solid wood under her feet; still she could not help thinking about how far it was to the ground below.

"There he is," said Jeremy, staring at the hole. "It's just the right time."

They inched their way along the limb. Mrs Frisby gripping the rough bark tightly, being careful not to stumble; and as they came closer, she could dimly perceive a shape like a squat vase sitting back in the hollow of the tree. Near the top of the vase, wide apart, two round yellow eyes glowed in the dark.

"He can't see us," Jeremy whispered. "It's still too light."

Perhaps not, but he could hear, for now a deep round voice, a voice like an organ tone, echoed out of the hollow trunk:

"Who is standing outside my house?"

Jeremy answered:

"Sir, I am a crow. My name is Jeremy. And I have brought a friend, I hope we have not disturbed you. My friend needs your advice."

"I see. And can your friend not speak for himself?"

"Sir, my friend is a lady, a lady mouse."

"A mouse?" The sonorous voice sounded unbelieving. "Why should a crow be a friend to a mouse?"

"I was trapped, sir, and she set me free. She saved me from the cat."

"That is possible," said the owl, "though unusual. I have heard of such a thing before. We all help one another against the cat."

"True. And now, sir, my friend herself is in trouble."

"I understand," said the owl, moving closer to the round entrance of his hollow. "Mrs Mouse, I cannot see you, for the glare of the daylight is too bright. But if you step inside my house, I will listen to what you have to say."

Mrs Frisby hesitated. She knew something of the dietary habits of owls, and did not much like the idea of being trapped in his house. Finally, she said timidly:

"Sir, I would not want to intrude. And I can hear you quite well from out here."

"Mrs Mouse, please understand that I have no interest at all, as a general rule, in helping mice to solve their problems. If you have indeed saved a bird from the cat, I will spare you a few minutes. But I do not discuss problems with people I cannot see. Either come inside, or tell your friend to take you home again."

Behind her, Mrs Frisby heard Jeremy whisper, very softly. "It's all right. He wouldn't harm you in his own home."

She whispered back, "I hope not." She walked up the limb to the hollow, climbed over the sill and stepped inside.

Up so close, the owl looked very large. Each of his feathery feet was tipped with five gleaming talons an inch long. His beak was curved and sharp and cruel. He blinked his yellow eyes and said:

"Please step across the room, away from the light."

Mrs Frisby did as she was told. As she grew accustomed to the dimness, she looked around her. The chamber into which she had stepped was spacious — at that level, almost half of the huge trunk was hollow — and clean, but the floor was extremely rough. It was not really a floor at all, but only the jagged ends of dead wood sticking up from below, like stalagmites in a cave, so that Mrs Frisby had to climb rather than walk as she crossed the room. At the back the walls narrowed to a corner, and there she saw that the owl had built himself a nest, as big as a water bucket, of twigs and leaves; from the top she could see protruding some wisps of the feathers with which he had lined it.

When she got near this nest, she stopped and faced the owl, who had turned from the light of the doorway and was peering at her with his great yellow eyes. Jeremy was nowhere to be seen. She could only hope he was still waiting on the limb outside.

"Now," said the owl, "you may state your problem."

Written by Robert C. O' Brien
Illustrated by Frances Cony

44

NIGHT

When the day is done
You see the last of the sun;
The children are in bed
Nightfall shrouds the earth
Everywhere seems to be dead;
The queen of sleep comes out
And so does the shrew with his little snout.
Flying in the air is the tiny bat
And on the ground is the cunning rat;
The owl hunting a mouse
While we are snug in the house;
The mole burrowing in the ground
And then at the surface he makes an earth mound.
The badger leaving his camouflage den,
While the fox is planning on stealing a hen;
At the eleventh hour
The crow is asleep at the top of the tower;
In the noonday night
A single sound gives you a fright.
The cock crows and dawn breaks,
And the night is here no more.

Richard McLaughlin
(aged 12)

How Birds Fly

Flight is motion through air. Birds achieve this by using their wings. When birds fly they have to overcome two things: *gravity* that pulls them down and *drag* caused by their bodies pushing through the air. Read on to find out how a bird's wings work and the clever ways in which the wings are used.

great tit

The shape of a bird's wing is very important. If you look at the side view of a wing you will see that it curves outwards on the top surface (**convex**) and it curves inwards on the lower surface (**concave**). This feature is very important in producing **lift** as described below.

Air moving *over* the wing can move away quickly and does not press heavily against it.

Less pressure above the wing and more pressure below it means that air pushes the wing (and bird) up. This is called LIFT.

Air moving *under* the wing is trapped by the curve and pushes upwards against it.

Powered or **flapping** flight uses a lot of energy and birds have powerful muscles. Strong fliers like ducks do not swim through the air as many people believe; they are actually **propeller driven**. The propellers — the long primary feathers — are at the tips of the wings.

The wing is twisted vertically to make as small a surface as possible to minimise drag.

At the top of the up-stroke the wing feathers begin to twist and spread to trap as much air under the wing as possible.

Gliding flight is when a bird moves forward in still air with its wings spread to create **lift**. Because of **drag**, it would gradually slow down so much that it would fall and so it must occasionally flap its wings or dive in order to pick up speed.

Soaring flight is used when a bird glides in air that is rising. **Thermals** are columns of air that rise, because they have been warmed by the land. Air can also rise when wind meets an obstruction, for example a cliff or a mountain. Birds that soar like this are broad-winged hawks, eagles, vultures and many seabirds. Over the open sea there are often **wind-currents** of different speeds and heights, one above the other. Some birds, like the albatross, spend most of their lives flying over the sea, gliding from one wind-current to another, only rarely flapping their wings.

herring gull

The sun's rays heat up the ground which then warms the air above it, causing it to rise.

wandering albatross

Wing feathers are held flat to make a large surface area on the *down-push*.

red-legged partridge

swift

hummingbird

sacred ibis

common buzzard

The type of wing a bird has depends on two things: the bird's need for **speed** and its need for **manoeuvrability**. Wings built for speed tend to be long and pointed, while short, broad wings are good for making sudden changes in direction.

IT'S A PLANE...
IT'S A BIRD...
IT'S ICARUS!

Who was Icarus?

Well, he wasn't Superman, that's for sure, because he made a botch of the whole business of flying. If only he'd listened to his dad! But then boys often don't.

Icarus and his father, Daedalus, are the main characters in an ancient Greek myth. It seems they lived on the island of Crete where Daedalus earned his living as a kind of inventor. He's said to have invented the saw, the axe and the gimlet (a small tool used for boring holes in wood or leather). One of his tasks was the construction of a maze, usually called the labyrinth, which acted as a prison for the horrible half-man, half-bull, creature called the Minotaur. Theseus, a mighty hero, eventually killed the Minotaur, thanks to a lot of help from Ariadne, the king's daughter. (It's a good story. Be sure to read it.) And who told Ariadne that Theseus should use a ball of wool to leave a trail as he went into the maze? None other than Daedalus, the inventor himself.

King Minos was furious when his monster was killed (it was very useful for frightening enemies and killing off people he didn't like) and as he couldn't punish Ariadne (who'd run off with Theseus), he promptly tossed Daedalus and his son into the maze instead. And posted guards at the entrance to make sure Daedalus didn't find the way out. But you can't keep a good man down! Daedalus looked at the sky and decided that the only way was up. So he set to work and made two sets of wings, using birds' feathers and wax. (Don't ask me where he got them from. The story doesn't say.)

Just before the escape Daedalus warned Icarus that he must not fly too close to the sun for fear the heat would melt the wax. Then up, up and away soared the pair. At first Icarus did as he was told. He flew an even course, not too close to the sea for fear the spray would wet the feathers and not too close to the sun. It was a wonderful feeling and soon he wanted to do all the things a bird does. He soared up . . . up, then swooped down . . . down. Spiralling like a hawk he sped up again, higher and higher, ignoring his father's cries. And of course, he went too high. The sun melted the wax. The feathers fell out. And Icarus plunged helplessly into the sea, while his anguished father flew on to lonely safety in Sicily.

THREE
ON THE WILDERNESS TRAIL

The three animals in this story have been staying away from their home while their owners are in England. Although treated well, all three have pined for their owners. When, by accident, they are left alone for a short time, Luath the labrador decides to set off for home, taking his companions, Bodger the bull terrier and Tao the Siamese cat with him. To reach home they will have to travel 450 kilometres across the north-western part of the great sprawling province of Ontario, Canada. It is a vast area of deeply wooded wilderness, a place of silence and solitude, where wild animals abound. When this part of their story starts they have been travelling for a day and a night and already the old bull terrier is in a bad way.

In the cold hour before dawn, the bull terrier woke, then staggered painfully to his feet. He was trembling with cold and was extremely hungry and thirsty. He walked stiffly in the direction of the pool nearby, passing on his way the cat, who was crouched over something held between his paws. The terrier heard a crunching sound as the cat's jaws moved, and, wagging his tail in interest, moved over to investigate. The cat regarded him distantly, then stalked away, leaving the carcass; but to the terrier it was a disappointing mess of feathers only. He drank long and deeply at the pool and on his return tried the feathers again, for he was ravenous; but they stuck in his gullet and he retched them out. He nibbled at some stalks of grass, then, delicately, his lips rolled back over his teeth, picked a few overripe raspberries from a low bush. He had always liked to eat domestic raspberries this way, and although the taste was reassuringly familiar, it did nothing to appease his hunger. He was pleased to see the young dog appear presently; he wagged his tail and licked the other's face, then followed resignedly when a move was made towards the direction of the road. They were followed a few moments later by the cat, who was still licking his lips after his feathery breakfast.

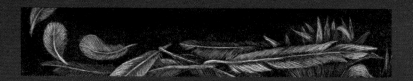

In the grey light of dawn the trio continued down the side of the road until they reached a point where it took a right-angled turn. Here they hesitated before a disused logging trail that led westward from the side of the road, its entrance almost concealed by over-hanging branches. The leader lifted his head and appeared almost as though he were searching for the scent of something, some reassurance; and apparently he found it, for he led his companions up the trail between the overhanging trees. The going here was softer; the middle was overgrown with grass and the ruts on either side were full of dead leaves. The close-growing trees which almost met overhead would afford more shade when the sun rose higher. These were all considerations that the old dog needed, for he had been tired today even before he started, and his pace was already considerably slower.

Both dogs were very hungry and watched enviously when the cat caught and killed a chipmunk while they were resting by a stream in the middle of the day. But when the old dog advanced with a hopeful wag of his tail, the cat, growling, retreated into the bushes with his prey. Puzzled and disappointed, the terrier sat listening to the crunching sounds inside the bushes, saliva running from his mouth.

A few minutes later the cat emerged and sat down, daintily cleaning his whiskers. The old dog licked the black Siamese face with his panting tongue and was affectionately patted on the nose in return. Restless with hunger, he wandered up the banks of the creek, investigating every rock and hollow, pushing his hopeful nose through tunnels of withered sedge and into the yielding earth of molehills. Sadly he lay down by an unrewarding blueberry bush, drew his paws down tightly over his blackened face, then licked the dirt off them.

The young dog, too, was hungry; but he would have to be on the verge of starvation before the barriers of deep-rooted Labrador heredity would be broken down. For generations his ancestors had been bred to retrieve without harming, and there was nothing of the hunter in his make-up; as yet, any killing was abhorrent to him. He drank deeply at the stream and urged his companions on.

The trail ran high over the crest of this hilly, wooded country, and the surrounding countryside below was filled with an over-whelming beauty of colour; the reds and vermilions of the occa-sional maples; pale birch, and yellow poplar, and here and there the scarlet clusters of mountain ash berries against a rich dark-green background of spruce and pine and cedar.

Several times they passed log ramps built into the side of the hill, picking their way across the deep ruts left by the timber sleighs below; and sometimes they passed derelict buildings in rank, overgrown clearings, old stables for the bush horses and living quarters for the men who had worked there a generation ago. The windows were broken and sagging and weeds were growing up between the floorboards, and one old rusted cookstove even had fireweed springing from the firebox. The animals, strangely enough, did not like these evidences of human occupation and skirted them as far as possible, hair raised along their backs.

Late in the afternoon the old dog's pace had slowed down to a stumbling walk, and it seemed as if only sheer determination were keeping him on his feet at all. He was dizzy and swaying, and his heart was pounding. The cat must have sensed this general failing, for he now walked steadily beside the dogs, very close to his tottering old friend, and uttered plaintive worried bleats.

Finally, the old dog came to a standstill by a deep rut half-filled with muddy water. He stood there as if he had not even the strength to step around it; his head sagged, and his whole body was trembling. Then, as he tried to lap the water, his legs seemed to crumple under him and he collapsed, half in and half out of the rut. His eyes were closed, and his body moved only to the long, shallow, shuddering breaths that came at widening intervals. Soon he lay completely limp and still. The young dog became frantic now: he whined as he scratched at the edge of the rut, then nudged and pushed with his nose, doing everything in his power to rouse the huddled, unresponsive body. Again and again he barked, and the cat growled softly and continuously, walking back and forth and rubbing his whole length against the dirty, muddied head. There was no response to their attention. The old dog lay unconscious and remote.

The two animals grew silent, and sat by his side, disturbed and uneasy; until at last they turned and left him, neither looking back — the Labrador disappearing into the bushes where the crack of broken branches marked his progress farther and farther away; the cat stalking a partridge which had appeared at the side of the trail some hundred yards away and was pecking unconcernedly at the sandy dirt. But at the shrill warning of a squirrel, it flew off across the trail with a sudden whirr into the trees, while the cat was still some distance away. Undaunted, still licking his lips in anticipation, the cat continued around a bend in the trail in search of another, and was lost to sight.

The shadows lengthened across the deserted track, and the evening wind sighed down it to sweep a flurry of whispering leaves across the rut, their brown brittleness light as a benison as they drifted across the unheeding white form. The curious squirrel peered in bright-eyed wonder from a nearby tree, clucking softly to itself. A shrew ran halfway across, paused and ran back; and there was a soft sound of wings as a whisky-jack landed and swayed to and fro on a birch branch, tilting his head to one side as he looked down and called to his mate to come and join him. The wind died away — a sudden hush descended.

Suddenly there was a sound of a heavy body pushing through the undergrowth, accompanied by a sharp cracking of branches, and the spell was broken. Chattering shrilly in alarm and excitement, the squirrel ran up the trunk of the tree and the whisky-jacks flew off. Now on to the trail on all fours scampered a half-grown bear cub, round furry ears pricked and small deep-set eyes alight with curiosity in the sharp little face as he beheld the old dog. There was a grunting snuffling sound in the bush behind the cub: his mother was investigating a rotten tree stump. The cub stood for a moment and then, hesitantly, advanced towards the rut where the terrier lay. He sniffed around, wrinkling his facile nose at the unfamiliar smell, then reached out a long curved black paw and tapped the white head. For a moment the mists of unconsciousness cleared, and the old dog opened his eyes, aware of danger. The cub sprang back in alarm and watched from a safe distance. Seeing that there was no further movement, he loped back and cuffed again with his paw, this time harder, and watched for a response.

Only enough strength was left in the old dog for a valiant baring of his teeth. He snarled faintly with pain and hatred when his shoulder was raked by the wicked claws of the excited cub, and made an attempt to struggle to his feet. The smell of the drawn blood excited the cub further; he straddled the dog's body and started to play with the long white tail, nibbling at the end like a child with a new toy. But there was no response: all conscious effort drained, the old dog no longer felt any pain or indignity. He lay as though asleep, his eyes veiled and unseeing, his lip still curled in a snarl.

Around the bend in the trail, dragging a large dead partridge by the wing, came the cat. The wing sprang back softly from his mouth as he gazed transfixed at the scene before him. In one split second a terrible transformation took place; his blue eyes glittered hugely and evilly in the black masked face, and every hair on the wheat-coloured body stood upright so that he appeared twice his real size; even the chocolate-coloured tail puffed up as it switched from side to side. He crouched low to the ground, tensed and ready, and uttered a high, ear-splitting scream; and, as the startled cub turned, the cat sprang.

He landed on the back of the dark furred neck, clinging with his monkeylike hind legs while he raked his claws across the cub's eyes. Again and again he raked with the terrible talons, hissing and spitting in murderous devilry until the cub was screaming in pain and fear, blinded with blood, making ineffectual brushing movements with his paws to dislodge the unseen horror on his back. His screams were answered by a thunderous roar as the huge black she-bear crashed through the bushes and rushed to the cub. She swiped at the clinging cat with a tremendous paw; but the cat was too quick for her and with a hiss of fury leaped to the ground and disappeared behind a tree.

The unfortunate cub's head received the full force of the blow and he was sent spinning across the track into the bushes. In a blind, frustrated rage, maddened by the cries of her cub, the mother turned for something on which to vent her fury, and saw the still figure of the old dog. Even as she lumbered snarling towards him the cat distracted her attention with a sudden leap to the side of the track. The bear halted, then reared up to full height for attack, red eyes glinting savagely, neck upstretched and head weaving from side to side in a menacing, snake-like way. The cat uttered another banshee scream and stepped forward with a stiff-legged, sideways movement, his squinting, terrible eyes fixed on his enormous adversary. Something like fear or indecision crept into the bear's eyes as the cat advanced; she shuffled back a step with lowered head. Slow, deliberate, purposeful, the cat came on — again the bear retreated, bewildered by the tactics of this terrible small animal, distraught by her cub's whimpering, slowly falling back before the relentless inch-by-inch advance. Now the cat stopped and crouched low, lashing his tail from side to side — the bear stopped too, shifting her weight uneasily before the spring that must follow, longing to decamp but afraid to turn her back. A sudden crackle of undergrowth turned the huge animal into a statue, rigid with apprehension — and when a great dog sprang out of the bush and stood beside the cat, teeth bared and snarling, every hair on his russet back and ruff erect, she dropped to all fours, turned swiftly and fled towards her cub. There was a last growl of desperate bravado from the bush and a whimpering cry; then the sounds of the bears' escape receded in the distance. Finally all was quiet again; the curious squirrel leaped from his ringside seat and scrambled farther down the trunk of the tree.

The cat shrank back to his normal size. His eyes regained their usual cool, detached look. He shook each paw distastefully in turn, glanced briefly at the limp, muddied bundle by his feet, blood oozing from four deep parallel gashes on the shoulder, then turned and sauntered slowly down the track towards his partridge.

The young dog nosed his friend all over, his lips wrinkling at the rank bear smell, then attempted to stanch the wounds with his rough tongue. He scratched fresh leaves over the bloodstained ones, then barked by the old dog's head; but there was no response, and at last he lay down panting on the grass. His eyes were uneasy and watchful, the hairs still stood upright in a ridge on his back, and from time to time he whined in perplexity. He watched the cat drag a large grey bird almost up to the nose of the unconscious dog, then slowly and deliberately begin to tear at the bird's flesh. He growled softly, but the cat ignored him and continued his tearing and eating. Presently, the enticing smell of raw, warm meat filtered through into the old dog's senses. He opened one eye and gave an appreciative sniff. The effect was galvanizing: his muddied half-chewed tail stirred and he raised his shoulders, then his forelegs, with a convulsive effort, like an old work horse getting up after a fall.

He was a pitiful sight—the half of his body that had lain in the rut was black and soaking, while the other was streaked and stained with blood. He looked like some grotesque harlequin. He trembled violently and uncontrollably throughout the length of his body, but in the sunken depths of the slanted black-currant eyes there was a faint gleam of interest—which increased as he pushed his nose into the still-warm bundle of soft grey feathers. This time there was no growling rebuff over the prey: instead, the cat sat down a few yards away, studiedly aloof and indifferent, then painstakingly washed down the length of his tail. When the end twitched he pinned it down with a paw.

The old dog ate, crunching the bones ravenously with his blunt teeth. Even as his companions watched him, a miraculous strength slowly seeped back into his body. He dozed for a while, a feather hanging from his mouth, then woke again to finish the last morsel. By nightfall he was able to walk over the soft grass at the side of the track, where he lay down and blinked happily at his companions, wagging his pitiful tail. The Labrador lay down beside him, and licked the wounded shoulder.

An hour or two later the purring cat joined them, carelessly dropping another succulent morsel by his old friend's nose. This was a deer mouse, a little creature with big eyes and long hind legs like a miniature kangaroo. It was swallowed with a satisfying gulp, and soon the old dog slept.

But the cat purring against his chest and the young dog curled at his back were wakeful and alert most of the remaining night; neither moved from his side.

Written by Sheila Burnford
Illustrated by Judith Selleck

On The Way To The Mission

They dogged him all one afternoon
  Through the bright snow,
Two white men, servants of greed;
He knew that they were there,
But he turned not his head;
He was an Indian trapper;
He planted his snow-shoes firmly,
He dragged the long toboggan
Without rest.

The three figures drifted
  Like shadows in the mind of a seer;
The snow-shoes were the whisperers
On the threshold of awe;
The toboggan made the sound of wings,
A wood pigeon sloping to her nest.
The Indian's face was calm.
He strode with the sorrow of fore-knowledge,
But his eyes were jewels of content
Set in circles of peace.

They would have shot him;
  But momently in the deep forest,
They saw something flit by his side:
Their hearts stopped with fear.
Then the moon rose.
They would have left him to the spirit,
But they saw the long toboggan
Rounded well with furs,
With many a silver fox-skin,
With the pelts of mink and of otter,
They were the servants of greed;
When the moon grew brighter
And the spruces were dark with sleet,
They shot him.

When he fell on a shield of moonlight
   One of his arms clung to his burden;
The snow was not melted:
The spirit passed away.

Then the servants of greed
   Tore off the cover to count their gains;
They shuddered away into the shadows,
Hearing each the loud heart of the other.
Silence was born.

There in the tender moonlight,
   As sweet as they were in life,
Glimmered the ivory features
   Of the Indian's wife.

In the manner of Montagnais women
   Her hair was rolled with braid;
Under her waxen fingers
   A crucifix was laid.

He was drawing her down to the Mission,
   To bury her there in the spring,
When the bloodroot comes and the windflower
   To silver everything.

But as a gift of plunder
   Side by side were they laid,
The moon went on with her setting
   And covered them with shade.

D. C. Scott
Illustrated by Greg Allen

OISIN
IN THE
LAND
OF
YOUTH

ISIN was one of the Fianna, a great race of warriors and heroes in Ireland in the dawn of history. He was also a singer and poet.

One day, Finn of the Fianna was out hunting with his men and Oisin was with them. But he stood apart watching the morning mists draw back from the silvery blue and the green and the grey of the lakes and the forests and mountains of Ireland. He loved the beauty of the land more than he cared for hunting.

As he gazed, he saw a rider on a white horse coming up a broad valley towards them. As the rider drew closer, he could see that it was a young woman. She had long, golden hair, her head was crowned with a glittering crown and she was richly dressed. There was silence among the men of the Fianna as she approached and she was the first to speak.

"I am Niav," she said. "I reign as princess in the Land of Eternal Youth and I have come in search of Oisin."

Oisin stepped forward, still staring. To his eyes, Niav had such brightness that she made all things dark around her.

"Your poems are known and your songs are sung in the Land of Youth," she told him. "Because of them I love you. My love has brought me across strange seas to find you. Will you come with me to the Land of Youth?"

Finn and his men did not move. A dream-like silence held them all. Oisin, unspeaking and enchanted by the blue eyes of Niav, mounted the white horse behind her.

Then Finn, in that moment, broke free from the spell. He took a step and tried to cry out. But Oisin's ears were deaf to him and, as he rode away with Niav, he only glanced back once.

The horse went so fast that tree, mountain and river blurred before Oisin's eyes. They came to the cliffs on the West coast of Ireland and beyond them the horse's hooves skimmed the white waves of the sea. Through sunlight and storm they rode until they reached the tall, gleaming towers of the Land of Youth. It was a country of murmuring streams and green fields bright with bird song. No storms visited it and no rough wind ever howled there.

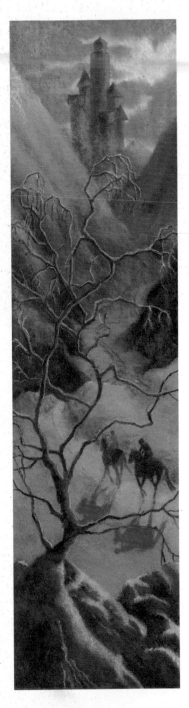

The king, the father of Niav, greeted Oisin and made him welcome.

"We are proud to have you here," he said, "for your poems and songs. And you, too, can be glad for here there is no sadness or growing old or dying and you can live here forever young."

A wedding feast had been arranged and Niav and Oisin were married in great splendour. So, Oisin's life was cloudless and happy, one day after another bringing him new delights. He could hunt and race horses and write songs and poems just as he had always enjoyed doing. But there, in that enchanted country, his joy in such things was always greater.

And yet there came a time when his sleep was visited by dreams. And these dreams were always of Ireland and the people and places he had known. He would wake from such dreams and walk the corridors of his castle with a troubled heart. But Niav was always there to turn his mind back to the pleasures of the Land of Youth. And, in his days of hunting, he forgot his dreams of the night.

One day, however, he and Niav had ridden on far ahead of the rest of his party and they found themselves on the edge of a grim, dark moor. As they halted, Oisin thought he heard, faint and far away, the sound of Finn's hunting horn. He set out across the moor to find where the call had come from and Niav followed.

They came in time to the high and frowning walls of a castle, built of black stone. By its great door loomed the entrance to a dungeon and in its depths Oisin could see a girl chained between two fierce eagles.

She called to him to ride away and save himself. The castle belonged to a giant called Fomor. He had held her prisoner there for longer than she could remember. He was fierce and cruel, killing all he came across and no one could defeat him in battle.

But Oisin rode up to the door and beat upon it with his axe. It opened and Fomor came out. He was hideous and mighty, armed with shield and sword and a massive spiked club. He roared his war cry and swung the club to split Oisin's skull. Oisin was too quick for him. He sprang aside then leapt in under Fomor's defences and his sword drew blood from Fomor's side. Enraged, Fomor attacked him furiously but he could not bring Oisin down. All day the struggle went on and it only ended when Oisin gave Fomor a deadly stroke as dusk fell.

The giant drew back into his castle and Oisin's wounds were cared for by Niav. Her magic powers healed them overnight. But Fomor's power was just as great. The next day he came out ready for the fight once more fresh and with no mark on him.

Seven days they fought and it was hard to choose between them who was the better fighter. But, at the end of each day, Oisin saw that one of the many chains that held the girl to her savage guards, the eagles, was loosed. Each night Oisin and Fomor were cured of their wounds and went each day unscarred and with new strength to their contest.

On the seventh day, things went against Oisin but he did not lose heart. It seemed as though Fomor would triumph. In that moment, though, Oisin gathered all his strength. His sword found the heart of his enemy and the giant fell with a crash.

The girl was free at last and the eagles turned to shadows and dwindled away. She thanked Oisin and left that dismal place to return to her own people and when Oisin had rested and was healed again, he and Niav began their journey home.

When they reached the borders of the gloomy moorland, they found themselves beside a wide and shining lake. Borne on the small waves that lapped the shore was a spear head attached to a broken shaft. Oisin got off his horse and picked it up.

It seemed to him that it had come from the world of mortal men. It looked like one of the ash spears that Finn and his men of the Fianna had used and Oisin's heart was full of yearning.

Seeing him standing there, sad-eyed, Niav tried to comfort him.

"I can see it reminds you of the world of men, my love," she said. "It would be better for you if you forgot it and thought rather of the Land of Youth where we are going and where there is no change or death or growing old. Then your heart would be light again."

"There is death on Earth," he said, "and growing old. But old age brings wisdom and after the woodland and the flowers have died in winter, the blossoms and the leaves come back to the trees in spring. It will be spring in Ireland now with the hawthorn white as foam and the golden daffodils blowing in the wind. I long to see them just once more, if only for a day."

"I cannot bear to see you unhappy," Niav sighed. "You can have your day in the world of men. Go back to Ireland. But let me warn you of your danger. Your foot must not touch the earth. You cannot walk on it now like a mortal man. Do not dismount from your horse but ride along and look at the spring."

He thanked her and kissed her, swearing that he would return, and rode away. She watched him go with sorrow in her eyes.

Ireland was as lovely as Oisin remembered it, though it had grown puzzling. Its people seemed smaller and its buildings looked different. He asked an old man for news of Finn and the Fianna and that was puzzling, too. The old man said that the only race he knew of that name had passed away. There had been a famous hero called Finn but he had been dead for over three hundred years.

So Oisin set out to look for the great walled fortress that Finn had held against all enemies. Perhaps he would find Finn there. But the walls of the fortress were broken and scattered so that no stone stood upon another and green moss covered them all.

Oisin saw that change had indeed come upon Ireland. It was time for him to return to the Land of Youth.

On his way he passed a stone quarry where men were struggling to lift out a huge slab of rock. Oisin's heart was moved to pity them. They seemed so much smaller and weaker than those men he had known in former times. Against the stalwart men of the Fianna, these seemed like children.

He drew up his horse alongside them and with one hand lifted out the slab for them. They cried out in admiration of his size and strength.

But bitter bad fortune was in that day for Oisin. The straps that held his saddle to his horse broke and he fell to the ground.

As he touched it, his bright brown hair turned white and his flashing eyes were suddenly dimmed with age. Three hundred years of mortal age came upon him in that moment so that he dwindled and died. In the wink of an eye all the glory and the strength that had been Oisin shrank to a skull and dry bones that looked like a bundle of sticks wrapped in rags and the workmen in the quarry were dumb with terror.

Written by Paul Groves and Nigel Grimshaw
Illustrated by Sophy Williams

FREEDOM RIDE

Andy, Christine, Lucy and Terry had been spending their holidays playing along the canal. The canal flowed around the old housing estate that was being pulled down and then into the river. One day, they discovered Dave, a young army deserter, hiding in one of the empty, derelict houses and before long were deeply involved in a plot to help him escape to a hideout on an island in the river.

They made a raft from oil drums and scraps of timber, but none of them expected the river to be so badly swollen from recent rains. At first, Dave had insisted that he should go alone, but the four children were not prepared to abandon either their friend or the adventure. Even Spotty Sally, the neighbourhood dog is determined to go along.

Andy continues the story ...

Dave was nearly crying. He shook his head. "Oh! he said. "What a bunch you are."

We started to drag the raft into the water. Dave stood there watching for a minute. Then he said, "O.K. But listen. I'm the captain of this boat. Right? Because I'm the oldest. So you must do exactly what I say. Is that agreed?"

We all cheered him, and he came to help us.

"We ought to have a name," I said. "We ought to have a name for our boat."

"O.K," said Dave. "What shall we call it?"

"Let's call it the *Jolly Roger*," said Terry.

"What about the *River Racer*?" said Lucy.

I thought and thought but I couldn't think of anything good.

"I know," said Christine. "This raft is going to help Dave escape, so let's call it *Freedom*."

"Yeah," I said. "That's a great name."

"O.K.," said Dave. "I name this raft *Freedom*, and good luck to all who ride on it."

We dragged *Freedom* into the river. Luckily it was quite slow at the side. We got it afloat and all clambered on board. We kept pushing Spotty Sally off because we didn't want her to come down the river, but she just swam after us and came on board again so we had to let her stay. Dave sat in the middle and gave orders. Spotty kept coming around and licking everybody in the face. Dave told which ones to paddle so that we always kept in the fast part of the current. He'd made the deck higher out of the water, but on the river there were all sorts of swirls and little waves, and with the splashing from the paddles, we got soaked through. The drizzle kept on. It was stinging my face like lots and lots of tiny needles. It was freezing, but no one complained of being cold because we were all proud of being on board *Freedom*.

Dave gave everybody food out of the pack that we had given him. At first we wouldn't take it because that was all he would have to live on, but it must have been after dinner time and we were starving, so in the end we all took some.

We didn't see anybody. We just passed between trees, all wet and leafy, and then fields with cows standing about eating. They were out in the rain all the time, and they never made a fuss. They didn't seem to mind at all, but I wished the rain would stop so I could get a bit warmer.

The river kept bending about. We had to keep crossing from side to side to stay with the fast current. If we got left on the wrong side we slowed down till we nearly stopped. When it was my side that had to paddle it was really hard work.

Suddenly we came around a bend and we were going towards where all these trees were leaning out right low over the water.

"Lucy and Chris, paddle! Paddle like mad! Andy and Terry, paddle backwards! Backwards! Faster! Come on, come on!" Dave shouted. But the river just carried us straight on towards the trees.

"Lie flat! Right down! Flat!" And I felt Dave's hand grab my arm, and Terry lying across my legs, and my head was crushed up against Dave's body. I could feel the cold of the water covering the deck and smell the strong smell of Dave's wet clothes. And then there was the swooshing and scraping of the leaves and branches over the front of the raft, and then over us. We were covered and brushed and dusted and scratched and hit. I yelled and closed my eyes. I could hear Dave's voice saying, "It's all right, kids. Hang on to the raft and hang on to each other." And then the swooshing passed over the back of the raft and the noise stopped. I opened my eyes and we all sat up.

"Are we all here?" said Dave. "Anybody get swept overboard?"

"I'm all scratched," said Christine. We all were.

"Where's Spotty?" yelled Lucy.

Spotty Sally wasn't on the raft. We looked back. All we could see was the heavy wet green curtain of the trees, brushing the frothing bubbling brown water that surged out from under it. But no Spotty Sally.

"Spotty!"

"Sally!"

"Sal!"

"Paddle backwards," said Dave. "Everybody. Paddle backwards as hard as you can to slow us down."

We paddled frantically and called and called, and then we saw the black face bob up this side of the trees. We paddled harder than ever and called louder.

"Spotty! Come on! Swim! Come on girl! Come on Sal!" She swam like mad and the river helped her shoot down towards us. We paddled backwards until she caught us. We dragged her on board and everyone cuddled her and stroked her and kissed her, even though she was soaking wet and cold, and nobody minded when she kept shaking herself all over us, or licking us in the eye or mouth.

It was all right for a bit after that. We passed the place where we usually went swimming. There were no people on the little sandy beach, but some cows had come down where we played, and they were standing with their feet in the water drinking from the river. They stopped drinking as we passed and looked at us. "They must think we're barmy," said Dave.

We sailed on quite a way further. I was just about frozen to death. The water was stinging my scratches. I was glad when I had to paddle because it helped me get a bit warmer. Then the bits of floorboard started to hurt my hands so much, I didn't want to paddle any more. I was really miserable and felt like crying. But nobody else cried or made a fuss, so I didn't either.

We came round a bend and there was a long straight stretch of river. The noise of the water seemed to be getting louder as we went along. And we seemed to be going faster. I looked down ahead and Dave was looking too. He got up on to his knees, and then stood up, so he could see better. I looked at his face. He was really worried. The noise was getting louder and we were gaining speed. We started going really fast then as though we were in a car and we'd changed into top gear. Up ahead the water was all broken up. All rough and bouncy. We accelerated even more and began bumping up and down.

"Andy and Terry! Paddle! Paddle, boys, as hard as you can! Chris, Luce, paddle backwards! Quick! Quick!"

"What's the matter, Dave? Is it a waterfall?" I said.

"No. It's rapids. Paddle now. Let's get over to the side."

But it was no use. We were just carried along. Faster and faster, and the noise became a roar. I was scared. I started to cry a little bit, but I tried not to let it show. Anyhow, I had rain all over my face, so no one could tell. I paddled as hard as I could even though my hands were hurting, but the raft just went plunging, like a bucking bronco, straight on.

"Give me that paddle!" Dave shouted. He pushed me into the middle of the raft. He started to paddle as hard as he could, but it didn't make any difference.

"Hang on to the raft!" he shouted. "Just hang on!" I grabbed hold of the edge of the deck, but as we bounced the oil drum smashed against my fingers. I yelled and let go. I was slung about the deck, sliding all over the place and bumping into people. Christine screamed out, "I've lost my paddle!"

"Don't worry. It doesn't matter. Just hang on!" Dave had stopped paddling too. We all just hung on and some of us were screaming. And then *crash* and then *crash* again, and then all the time, *bang, bang, bang*, and we all started yelling.

"It's all right," yelled Dave. "It's all right. Really. We're just banging on the rocks on the bottom of the river. That just means it's shallow. That means we're safe."

But he didn't convince anybody. The banging went on. And we all went on crying. And then Christine did a terrible loud scream. "Dave!" she yelled. Dave had jumped off the side of the raft and was in the water. He was hanging on to the raft and being dragged along.

"I'm making it lighter," he yelled, "so it doesn't bang so much". But it went faster still and he had to drag himself back on board. Then Terry screamed out and kept on screaming. No one knew what was the matter. "It's all right," Dave kept saying. "It's all right." But Terry just pointed and kept on. Then we saw what he was yelling about. One of our oil drums was floating off down the river in front of us, like a wheel that's fallen off your car when you're going flat out, and it was going even faster than we were. It had been the one that Terry had been sitting on. He just felt it bounce away, and he gripped onto the raft, but he thought it was all breaking up. The water poured and splashed all over us, and the river roared, and the raft was tipped down at one corner now.

Bang, bang, bang, CRASH! We screamed, we didn't know what was happening. The icy water was pouring over us, but we were still hanging on to the raft, which was tipped up more than ever. But the banging had stopped. And we were still. It took a little while to realise it. What had happened was that we'd struck against a huge rock, and wedged. Terry and Lucy and Dave were down in the water with just their heads sticking out like seals. But Christine and me were just up to our waists. Spotty Sally kept scrabbling up and sliding down again over and over.

"Where's the stuff?" yelled Lucy. I could see Dave's rucksack floating away at top speed, and some of the food bags, but not the hammer and radio and everything.

"Never mind about that." said Dave. "Just as long as we're all safe." Well, I didn't feel very safe stuck there in the middle of this river, with icy water bursting all over me at about a hundred miles an hour, but I didn't say anything. Dave was talking loud in a very calm voice.

"Now listen," he said. "Please, please, let's have no more screaming and crying. It won't help. Everybody's safe. Nobody's hurt. Everything's going to be all right. We're in a difficult position, and we've got to think quietly and calmly about what's the best thing to do. Now please. It doesn't help to scream at a time like this. Keep calm and everything will be all right."

Dave looked around at the river for a bit. Then at the bank. "Right," he said. "We're quite close to this side. I'll try it out first to see if it's all right. Then I'll come back and get you. Now just hang on to the raft."

He got hold of a rock sticking out of the water with one hand, and lowered himself into the river. As he took his weight off the raft, it began to lift up in the water, and we all screamed again. "It's all right," said Dave. "Sit tight." Then, sitting on the edge of the raft, he dipped into the water like a duck feeding, and came up with rocks off the river bed that he could hardly lift. He heaped rocks onto the raft and then he carefully got off again. This time the raft stayed where it was. The water was rushing by at terrific speed making a really loud roaring noise like a giant machine. There were rocks sticking up everywhere, like river monsters poking their heads out of the water to watch us. The rushing water divided around them and swelled up into waves like you get in a rough sea.

Dave let go of the raft and stepped into the current, and then he just got swept away. He just disappeared. Then we saw him bobbing up and down, bouncing over rocks, and being thrown in and out of the angry rushing river, as it carried him along like an old piece of broken wood. He struggled and struggled, but it didn't make any difference. The river was in charge. And the monsters just stood and watched. Christine shouted out, "Daaaaave!" in a long-drawn-out scream that made my hair stand on end. By the time she got to the end of it, Dave was a hundred yards downstream and we could hardly see him. Just a glimpse of his green anorak. But we could see he was getting closer to the bank.

He climbed ever so slowly up the bank, like in a slow-motion film, as if he was very heavy and it was painful for him to move. Then he knelt up and waved to us. We waved back, relieved that he wasn't drowned, partly for him and partly for us. After a moment he got up and began to hobble along the bank towards us as fast as he could. He fell down about four or five times. Lucy yelled out, "Good old Dave," and we all waved. We just had to sit there in the water till he got level with us. He shouted to us but we could hardly hear him above the roar of the water. I think he was saying, "Just hang on!" and something else.

Then he hobbled further upstream past us. I thought he was going to go away and leave us. I got a pain as though strong icy fingers had got hold of whatever I've got inside my stomach, and had twisted them up. I shouted to him but he couldn't hear. Then he made his way down the bank to the edge of the water by sliding on his backside. He stood up, and suddenly threw himself out into the river again. He swam wildly, as though he was trying to swim across to the other bank, but he was being swept down the river sideways. He was trying to get far enough out to reach us before the river brought him down to us. We all yelled, "Come on, Dave! Come on, Dave!" But he was being carried down too fast. As he came level he gave up swimming and reached out his hands, and I saw his eyes scared and his mouth open and the river water gushing into his face. I stretched out to him but I couldn't reach him and he was past. But then he jolted up against a rock, and he threw his arms around it. The river was trying to carry his legs away and he struggled against the water. It looked as though he was wrestling with this big river monster. Gradually he managed to haul himself to his feet and drag himself onto the raft. We hugged each other all at once. Even Spotty Sally tried to join in the hugging. But we soon realised that we were right back as we were when we first crashed.

"I've got a new respect for water," Dave said. "I never believed it could be so strong."

Written by Nigel Gray

SOUND TRAVEL

Did You Know...

... that when someone next to you taps a biro on the desk, it's not the sound that travels to your ear? What's happening is that the movement of the biro is disturbing the air, it's making it shake or vibrate. These vibrations are travelling along through the air until they meet your ear drums. They make them vibrate too. Your ear immediately converts the vibrations into electrical signals to your brain, telling you that you hear a sound.

And what you probably say is, "Please stop that noise, I can't think!"

Heavy As Air!

Sound needs something solid through which to travel. And if you're thinking that air isn't solid, you're wrong! It mightn't seem so when you're breathing in great gulps of it, but air definitely has mass. All those tiny particles of gas and water vapours that make up the air molecules in our atmosphere are really pretty solid. Still doubtful? Here's an experiment to prove it. Try blocking one end of a bicycle pump and then pushing in the handle. The minute you let go, the handle will spring back as the squashed air returns to its original volume. It's elastic, but it's solid.

Can You Hear Me?

Early Roman writings tell us that the mighty Persian ruler, Cyrus, built lines of signal towers, radiating out from his capital city. From the top of each one, men with powerful voices shouted messages to the next tower. They used a special call, rather like yodelling and sent the messages word by word. (Obviously you'd have to have good hearing as well as a loud voice to get the job. Wonder how many messages got muddled?)

Try These:

Experiments that show how sound moves through the air.

1 Tie one end of a skipping rope to a wall and stand back far enough so the rope can be shaken. Now flick that end and you'll notice a ripple moving along the rope. The piece you flicked doesn't move, but the movement or vibration does. That's the way sound travels through air.

2 Set out several billiard balls in a row so they are all touching each other. Roll another of these balls against the ball at one end of the row. Each ball in turn is squeezed or bumped when hit, so that it passes on the pressure to the next ball before it relaxes again. Finally, the last ball in the row rolls out because it has only the air to pass the pressure on to. Can you see now how a sound wave travels by particles of air bumping and to-and-fro-ing against each other in a movement that starts when the first particles are made to vibrate?

Slow Traveller

Compared with light, sound travels very slowly. It takes air waves 3 seconds to travel one kilometre, but light can zip across the same distance in just .000003 seconds. That's a million times faster!

Now Hear This!

The Greeks and Romans both experimented with giant speaking tubes or megaphones, which were supposed to be able to send the human voice over a distance of 18 km, but there's no evidence to prove this. In 1670 however, English inventor Sir Samuel Moreland demonstrated a special megaphone he'd made to King Charles II. Apparently he was able to be heard at a distance of over 2 km. *Know how a megaphone makes your voice sound louder?*
It's trumpet-like shape stops the sound from spreading out. It directs it and amplifies it.

Thunder and Lightning

When a storm appears to be raging just above your house, try timing the delay between the flash of lightning and the roll of thunder. Although both occur at the same time, the sound takes longer to reach you than light does. A 6-second delay? The storm is 2 km away. If the time between the two gets shorter and shorter, the storm is getting closer. If the delay is longer, you know the storm is moving away.

FASCINATING FACTS ABOUT SOUND

Watery Echoes

Sound is seldom used for measuring distances on land, but it's very useful under water. A ship equipped with an echo sounder, can send out a burst of sound waves from its hull and more or less bounce these off the sea bed. By timing the delay between the original signal and the reflection or echo back from the bottom, it's possible to calculate how far it is to the sea bed and to work out the depth of the water. These sound reflections are used to produce images on the screen of a cathode-ray tube. (It's similar to the one in your TV set.) From this, a "sound map" of the area beneath the ship can be plotted. It's also possible, using something called a Plan Position Indicator (PPI for short) to work out the distance and direction of other ships nearby. Fishing boats can use this technique to locate shoals of fish.

Sound You Can't Hear

Ultrasonic vibrations are ones that are above the range that can be picked up by human ears. A dog can hear sounds its owner can't, for instance and it's believed that sea animals communicate through these very high frequencies.

Ultrasonics have been used as a basis for communication devices in submarines since World War II and are now being put to use in many different ways. For instance, flaws inside metal objects can be reflected on a screen and doctors have found that a picture of an unborn baby produced by ultrasonic reflections is much safer for both child and mother than an X-ray.

Sonic Boom

When a fast-flying jet moves through the air, the pressure on its nose builds up, but as long as the plane is not flying above the speed of sound, these pressure waves stay well ahead of it.

However, if the plane approaches the speed of sound, it catches up with these pressure waves and once they are unable to escape from the aircraft, they build up to form a shock wave. This moves along with the aircraft, spreading out behind it to form a cone of intense high pressure. At this point people down below hear a loud bang or sonic boom.

I'm so glad they can't listen in on our private conversations ....

A READING LIST
FOR THOSE ABOUT TO START ON FEARFUL JOURNEYS

Parachute Jumping	by Willie Maykit
On the Rocks	by Mandy Lifeboat
Escape to the Bush	by L'ostin D. Woods
At the North Pole	by I. C. Blast
At the South Pole	by Ann Tartic
The Tiger's Revenge	by Claud Body
Road Transport	by Laurie Driver
Jungle Fever	by Amos Quito
A Clifftop Tragedy	by Eileen Dover
Stranded on the Motorway	by Buster Tyre
In the Lion's Den	by Norah Bone
So Tired	by Carrie Mee
The Cannibal's Daughter	by Henrietta Mann
The Earthquake	by Major D. Zaster
Snow Fall	by Ava Lanche
There and Back	by Carmen N. Gowan

JAN VAN DER LOO

FIGHT TO THE DEATH?

WRITTEN BY DOUGLAS HILL • ILLUSTRATED BY AZOO

The time is far into the future. It is long after the world was almost destroyed by nuclear disaster. The world has since been invaded by alien Slavers, a fearsome race who prey on people. Now, those few humans who survived the nuclear disaster live primitive lives in isolated villages.

Finn Ferral was found as a baby in the forest, by Josh Ferral. One day when Finn is out hunting, the Slavers attack his village and carry off old Josh and his daughter Jena. Thus begins an incredible and dangerous journey as Finn sets out to find and rescue his adopted family. He is armed with just his knife and the heatlance which he managed to capture from a group of Slavers.

Finn is cooking a couple of fish over an open fire. It is his evening meal. The forest is dark and gloomy all around him. Suddenly, he hears something moving, something large, for the sound of rustling branches and crunching twigs indicate a creature big and fearless enough not to have to care much about being silent.

The bear, or whatever it was, had drawn closer now, moving in a semi-circle around the small pond. Pulling his fish, now cooked, off the fire, Finn set them aside to cool a little, and kept a careful watch on the foliage in the direction of the sounds.

There—a bush trembled slightly. Finn did not look directly at it, but kept it in view from the corner of his eye as he leaned forward to pick up one of the fish.

As he did so, the creature that had been moving so noisily among the trees emerged into full view from behind the bush.

Not a bear. Not any other kind of animal.

It was the bulky, half-naked shape of a beast-man of the Slavers— with a glare that seemed to mingle both surprise and fury in its shadowed, deep-set eyes.

For an instant Finn was rigid with shock. And the beast-man also remained still, studying Finn.

The creature was not tall, but was enormously broad and powerful, stooping slightly, with a jutting hump of muscle on its upper back just below the thick neck. It wore baggy leggings and heavy, knee-high boots, and a long-bladed weapon like a machete was strapped in a leather sheath at its back, the hilt thrusting up above a massive shoulder.

The naked upper body was covered with long, shaggy hair that was light in colour, almost yellow, and the face was mostly hidden in a massive dark beard. The heavy jut of the eyebrows made the eyesockets seem like caves, yet the forehead was oddly high, seeming more so because the hair on the creature's head was thinning and receding.

And that forehead was furrowed deeply, as the creature took a wary step forward.

Finn, scrambling up, brought the heatlance with him. The beast-man's eyes widened as it saw the weapon. It halted, crouching as if to leap back. And Finn raised the lance, his thumb stabbing at the shallow groove that fired it.

The tip of the metal rod glowed scarlet. But there was nothing more. No lethal ray of heat flared out.

Frantically Finn glanced down, jabbing again and again at the firing groove. Still nothing. And whatever was wrong with the weapon, it was too late for Finn to discover it.

With surprising speed for a creature of its bulk, the beast-man swept the machete from the sheath at its back. The cruel blade glittered as the creature lunged forward, mouth agape in a bestial snarl.

Finn's knife still lay on the grass, beside the fire, and there was no time for the sling. Gripping the useless lance like a club, he crouched, bracing himself to meet the monstrous charge. They came together like two savage beasts—Finn with the quick and agile ferocity of a cougar, the beast-man with the bulk and power of a maddened bear.

The machete hissed in a looping swing at Finn's head, then clanged resoundingly as Finn struck the blow aside with the heatlance. Again the machete slashed down, seeming weightless in the beast-man's great fist. Finn ducked aside, swinging the lance in a counter-blow that grazed the beast-man's ribs.

So they fenced, stroke and counter-stroke, with Finn mostly on the defensive against the murderous blade of the machete. Several times that deadly edge nicked Finn's jerkin, slicing into the tough leather as if it were paper. But more often Finn remained quick enough to stay out of reach of the flashing blade. And some of his blows found their marks, too—though the solid thump of the lance against the beast-man's belly or leg seemed to have no effect whatever.

The fight lasted only moments, as the two circled, swayed and struck. It was the beast-man who changed tactics first. A chopping blow at Finn's side became a feint, followed by a crushing kick. But Finn dodged the huge boot, and lashed out fiercely with the lance at the hand that held the machete.

Metal struck a hairy wrist, and the beast-man bellowed as the machete flew from its grasp. Swift as a striking snake, Finn swung the lance around, aiming for his opponent's head. But the beast-man's speed had not been impaired. A vast hand flashed up, clutched the lance—and with awesome, easy power wrenched it from Finn's grasp and flung it away.

Then the monster lunged at Finn's throat.

Like a crazed wildcat Finn fought, with fists and knees and feet. Some of his blows brought deep grunts, but otherwise had no more effect on the beast-man than they would have had on the bole of a tree. The terrible hands gripped Finn's jerkin, dragging him off balance. Locked together in combat, the two toppled to the ground—Finn beneath the beast-man.

All the breath was driven from Finn's lungs by the impact, with the beast-man's enormous weight crushing him. Half-stunned, he could only writhe and twist helplessly as mighty hands and knees pinned him firmly to the ground.

At last he let his body sag, knowing there was no escape, and stared up at the bestial face, waiting for death.

But to his surprise, there was no look of triumph or brutal murderousness on the beast-man's face. Instead, there was something oddly like a crooked smile on the beard-veiled mouth, and something like a twinkle in the deep-set eyes.

"Now then."

Finn blinked in surprise. The beast-man's voice was not like the snarling, barking sound of the others of his kind that Finn had fought. It was deep and rich, rolling like melodious thunder from the depths of the great barrel chest.

"Now then," the creature repeated. "If you're all through tryin' to kill me, maybe we can have ourselves a little conversation."

the Walkie-Talkie

To give it its proper name, it's a hand-held transceiver — an amazing invention that has helped save the lives of many people when their journeys have turned into nightmares.

When disaster strikes, the awful fear is that you'll be lost, cut off from communication with anyone. It can be worse if someone with you is hurt and needs urgent medical help. Once there was no solution but to stay put and hope that help would arrive in time. Many have died alone and afraid because they had no way of calling for help. This can still happen of course, but now the advice to people embarking on a lonely journey is: CARRY A HAND-HELD TRANSCEIVER!

When was it invented? During World War II. It meant that troops in the frontline and the rearguard could communicate with each other, quickly and easily.

What's so good about it?
- it's a two-way radio — you can use it to send *and* receive messages.
- it can transmit messages over distances of roughly 1–5 km. (Some very specialised models have a range many times this — up to hundreds of kms and more!)

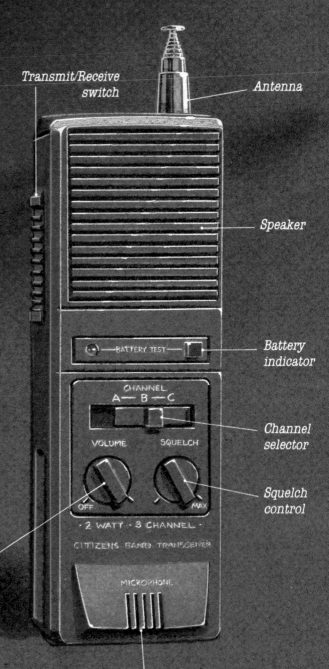

Transmit/Receive switch

Antenna

Speaker

Battery indicator

CHANNEL
A — B — C

Channel selector

VOLUME   SQUELCH

Squelch control

OFF   MAX

· 2 WATT · 3 CHANNEL ·

CITIZENS BAND TRANSCEIVER

Volume control

MICROPHONE

Microphone

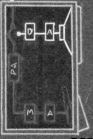

TRANSMIT

- it uses micro-chips, so it's small and light.
- you can carry it anywhere because it doesn't depend on cords and lines like the telephone.
- it's strong, durable and cheap!

Who uses it? Lots of people, including police, firemen, emergency workers, bushwalkers and boaters. And, of course, the military.

How does it work?

1 You speak into the microphone which changes your voice into an electric current.
2 The amplifier (A) increases the level of the tiny electric current.
3 The modulator (M) alters the current so the signals are transmitted on the correct frequency.
4 The power amplifier (PA) strengthens the signals.
5 The signals move through the air like waves and are picked up by the antenna on the other walkie-talkie.
6 The demodulator (D) changes the signals back into an electric current.
7 The amplifier (A) increases the level of these currents to make them usable by the speaker.
8 The speaker changes the electric current back into the sound of your voice which carries your voice to the ears of the listener.

All within a fraction of a second! Amazing!

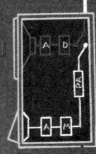

RECEIVE

A = amplifier
M = modulator
PA = power amplifier
AT = antenna
D = demodulator

The Hodja's Funeral

A TRADITIONAL TALE FROM TURKEY.
Adapted by **PAT EDWARDS** and illustrated by **PETER FOSTER**

Once there lived in Turkey a foolish fellow whom everyone called the Hodja. One day he was up in a tree cutting wood.

Hey, there, friend! You'll fall down if you go on chopping like that!

CHIP!

CHOP!

88

So the Hodja sat down in the shade with his hand on his heart to see if it were still beating. After awhile the hungry donkey got tired of waiting.

The sound of the donkey's bray filled the Hodja with terror.

I'M DEAD! I'M DEAD!

And the foolish fellow lay down beside the road and shut his eyes. After a time a group of villagers passed by.

LOOK! LOOK! It's the Hodja!

They were not much brighter than the Hodja.

Poor fellow! I think he's **DEAD!**

We'd better get a coffin.

They fetched a coffin from the village and laid the Hodja in it.

How sad his family will be!

Now I'm at eternal rest!

Come on, let's carry him home.

Never knew him well, but he looks nice fellow.

91

On the road through the forest, they came to a crossroads.

The villagers, angry at being tricked stamped off.

And the Hodja was forced to face the fact that he still had to make his journey through life and that there was still work to do.

93

Journey to the Pole of Impossibility

Written by Osmar White   Illustrated by Jeff Hook

"Hush, McGurk", said the other members of the Explorers Club. "You must be daft. Nobody will ever discover the Pole of Impossibility. The South Pole was discovered years ago and so was the Magnetic Pole. But the Pole of Impossibility is *impossible*. The idea of riding a camel down there is *absurd*!"

People with no imagination never bothered the bravest explorer of modern times, the great Alistair Angus Archibald McGurk. Riding his remarkable double-humped camel, Cathie Khan, and with his trusty husky Trotsky, he travels to Antarctica, determined to be the first to reach the Pole of Impossibility.

But instead of ice, snow and freezing cold, they travel through a land that is hot and steamy, with fat black clouds overhead.

Having at last struggled up the side of a very steep hill they discover what is causing these unexpected weather conditions.

When at last they reached the top, the long, hard climb turned out to be worth their effort. The view from the heights was terrific!

Dr McGurk pulled out his high-powered telescope and looked all around. Almost at once he saw what was causing the mysterious black clouds and this strange oasis in the desert of ice.

Far far away to the south a great volcano rose from the horizon. A column of smoke drifted lazily from its crater and spread out like a mushroom in the sky.

Dr McGurk was so excited he nearly fell off Cathie's hump. Then he remembered the real purpose of his expedition — to reach the Pole of Impossibility. Discovering new volcanoes wasn't nearly so important as getting to the Pole. He dismounted from his camel, took his sextant out of his sporran, and started to make observations and calculations. He had to make sure that he was headed in *exactly* the right direction.

Explorers have to be very good at navigating with the help of a sextant, so it didn't take Dr McGurk long to make another discovery. A discovery which gave him a terrible shock.

THE POLE OF IMPOSSIBILITY WAS RIGHT ON TOP OF THE SMOKING VOLCANO!

After doing the observations and calculation all over again to be quite sure he hadn't made a mistake, the brave Scotsman sat on a rock to think things over. He knew it would be awfully dangerous to go right to the Pole. If the volcano erupted properly and spurted out red-hot rocks and lava, he would be fried to a frizzle and a crisp and never live to tell the tale.

Dr McGurk's courage almost failed him. But then he called to mind the last words of his father, the late Lord Magnus McGurk of Ben Lomond.

The old laird had died many years before at the age of 103, after being bucked off his horse at the Edinburgh Tattoo. Before he passed away, he called his son to his bedside and whispered, "Dinna ever forget, young Alastair, that nothing is impossible for a McGurk. It just takes us a wee bittie longer!"

Inspired by this memory, Dr McGurk jumped to his feet and shouted, "Up, up and awa, my bonnie beasties! On to the Pole! We'll never tur-r-rn back the noo!"

The plain from which the great volcano rose up was an eerie, spooky place. It was watered by rivers and lakes and fountains. But they were very different from any rivers and lakes and fountains Dr McGurk had ever seen. The water in them was boiling. Some of the fountains spouted steam, every hour on the hour, and some of the rivers ended in lagoons of bubbling mud.

The ground was pimpled with fuming fumaroles — holes that belched out smoke and sulphur and horrid smells brewed up in the bowels of the earth.

There were blow-holes that blew molten brimstone, and mudholes with bubbles that went "Plop" most of the time and "Poop" some of the time. There were even rigmaroles that went on and on all of the time.

Their final sprint towards the Pole of Impossibility exhausted Dr McGurk and his animals. Cathie sank to her knees groaning and grumbling when at last they reached the foot of the volcano, and Trotsky flung himself down beside a blow-hole with his tongue hanging out.

They were all too tired and weak to start climbing the mountain that day. Dr McGurk pitched the tent on the safest spot he could find and sat down to eat a slice of cold

haggis by the banks of a mud pool. He had just finished his supper and was enjoying a drop of Highland Dew when, without warning, a horrible looking *thing* rose from the steamy swamp in front of him.

The creature had round fishy eyes as big as saucers, two huge yellow tusks, and long drooping whiskers from which the mud dripped down in the most revolting way.

"Oh, erk!" shrieked Dr McGurk. "Oh, yuk! It's a muddy dinosaur!"

To his even greater alarm, a deep voice behind him said, "Take it easy, stranger. That ain't no dinosaur. That's only old Elemenopee, the lady walrus in my party, having her beauty bath. That walrus wouldn't hurt a fly. No, sir!"

Dr McGurk whirled around and found himself face to face with a small hairy man with short legs, fat feet and long arms. He had tiny eyes like aniseed balls and bristly black eyebrows like scrubbing brushes.

The hardy Scotsman's heart sank into his boots. He thought, "So I'm not the first man to reach the Pole of Impossibility, after all. The Americans have beaten me to it." He was bitterly disappointed, but like all brave men he was a good loser.

"How do ye do, sir," he said stiffly. "I am Dr Alastair Angus Archibald McGurk MD, I am a member of the Royal Exploring Society, London, England. You are the leader of the American Expedition to the Pole of Impossibility, I presume."

The small hairy man looked puzzled. He shook his head. "Nope," he said. "Don't know nothin' about no Pole of Impossibility. And I wouldn't be an American for all the oil in Arabia. The name is Yeti, Doc. I'm right proud to meet a Britisher. I'm from Tibet, myself. Shake!"

They shook hands, but Dr McGurk was suspicious. He had heard the name Yeti before, but for the moment he couldn't remember where.

"Excuse me, Mr Yeti," he said, "but if you're a native of Tibet, why do you speak with such a strong American accent? You sound just like a cowboy in a television film."

"Don't rightly know why I talk like a cowboy, Mac," the hairy man said. "It could be because I've watched so much television. Or it could be because I worked for a dame called Eskimo Nell in Alaska, after I left home in the Himalaya Mountains."

Suddenly Dr McGurk's memory worked. The Himalaya Mountains. Of course! "I've got it!" he cried. "I know who you are. You're an Abominable Snowman!"

The hairy man looked furious. "Stranger," he said coldly, "them's fightin' words. I ain't 'bominable — and what's more I ain't a man! All us Yetis resigned from the human race, 'way back in BC, when the Chinese invented gunpowder and started blowin' folks up with it."

Without another word, the Yeti turned on his heel and shambled away. Soon he disappeared in a cloud of smoke from one of the rigmaroles.

When Dr McGurk looked back towards the mud pool, the walrus had vanished, too.

That night the explorer couldn't get to sleep for a long while. He was worried. He thought the fumes from the fumaroles must be poisonous and were giving him hallucinations — making him see things that weren't really there. He couldn't believe that the Yeti and the walrus were real.

All the books Dr McGurk had read about Nature said that walruses lived only in the cold seas near the North Pole, and Abominable Snowmen lived only on Mount Everest.

However, he was so tired that when he dropped off at last he slept deeply and awoke only when Cathie licked his nose with her rough tongue to remind him that it was time for breakfast.

After his good rest Dr McGurk felt much more cheerful. He poked his head out of the tent and looked around. The volcano was still smoking away quietly and the lakes and rivers weren't boiling any faster than they had the day before. "Och, aye," the determined Scotsman said to himself. "I'd better climb the mountain to the Pole right away and get the job over with."

He was putting on his climbing boots when, all at once, Trotsky started to make a dreadful racket outside. He barked and howled and yipped and yowled and then burst into the tent rubbing his nose with his front paws.

At first Dr McGurk thought the poor dog had burned his nose sniffing at a red-hot fumarole. But when he looked more closely he saw it was bleeding from a deep scratch.

"Good grief!" the explorer exclaimed. "If the idea wasna so daft, I'd say you'd been chasing a cat."

At that very moment an awful smell drifted into the tent. "Phew!" gasped Dr McGurk, holding his own nose and feeling quite ill, "Who cad be bakig thad terrible pog?"

Once more he poked his head out of the tent and saw what it was. A big, black cat with white spots was sitting on a nearby rock, washing its whiskers. "Scat!" Dr McGurk shouted, waving his arms. "Awa' with ye! Scram, ye fetid feline!"

Then, to his amazement, he saw the Abominable Snowman striding towards him angrily.

"Cool it, Mac," the Yeti snapped. "You've got no right to call a poor, harmless polecat names. Sure he stinks a bit, but that camel of yours is no bunch of violets, neither."

"Oh grief, oh woe," Dr McGurk groaned. "I thought you were an *hallucination*. But you're *real*!"

"Sure I'm real," the Abominable Snowman said. "And if you ever let that mangy mongrel of yours chase Ponsonby again, I'll show you how real I am!"

Dr McGurk still couldn't believe his eyes and ears — or his nose.

"It canna be true, it canna. It's no' natural," he muttered.

"What's not natural?" the Yeti asked crossly.

Dr McGurk felt quite dizzy with shock. "Mr Yeti," he said, "would you mind very much if I *touched* you?"

"Why do you want to touch me?" the Abominable Snowman demanded.

"Because if I touched you and found you were really there, I could believe in you," Dr McGurk replied.

"Very well. Okay," the Yeti said. "I don't like folks touchin' me, but I'll let you. Just once."

Dr McGurk reached out and poked the Yeti's stomach. Yes, he was real. His stomach felt just like a football with fur on it.

"Do you want to touch my polecat, too?" the Abominable Snowman asked.

"If you don't mind, I'd rather not," Dr McGurk murmured politely, "but may I take your photograph?"

"Why?"

"Because people will believe I have really seen a Yeti if I have a photograph of you. They won't just take my word for it," Dr McGurk explained.

The Yeti scratched his head. "I'll have to think about that, Mac," he said. "But I can't wait now. I'm too busy today. I've gotta wash the mud off my walrus and find my polar bear. Percival's wandered off again, the pesky varmint. See you later."

Dr McGurk gave up trying to imagine what a Yeti, a walrus, a polar bear and a polecat were doing near the Pole of Impossibility — or how they could possibly have got there. He felt dizzy again and sat down until his head cleared and his confidence came back.

Then the intrepid Scot leapt to his feet and gave the dreaded battle cry of the Clan McGurk. "Whirra-whirroo, hurray, hurroo!" he roared. "Up the McGurks! On to the Pole!"

The climb to the top of the great volcano on which the Pole of Impossibility stood was even harder and more dangerous than Dr McGurk had feared.

The ascent took sixteen hours and twelve minutes, and several times the climbers narrowly escaped being buried by avalanches of hot ashes and pumice-stones.

Once a glowing ember fell on Cathie's coat and Dr McGurk had to beat it out with his hat to stop her bursting into flames. The faithful animal thought he was spanking her unjustly. Her lips trembled and she burst into tears.

At last the gallant trio reached the lip of the crater and looked down into the lake of molten lava far below.

Was the Pole of Impossibility down there in those dreadful depths? If it was, Dr McGurk knew that he would never be able to reach it alive.

Dr McGurk did more observations and calculations and discovered that the Pole of Impossibility must be on a high point of the crater about one hundred metres from where he was standing. He couldn't see very clearly because the smoke got in his eyes and made him sneeze and splutter so painfully that he thought he would be forced to retreat before he could actually find the Pole.

Trotsky, of course, found the Pole. If there is a pole about, dogs will always find it. They have an instinct for such things.

Dr McGurk ran across, scrambled to the top and shouted "Whirra-whirroo!" again. Then he took the flag of Free Scotland out of his sporran, waved it three times around his head and took possession of everything he could see in the name of the late Bonnie Prince Charlie.

Life in the ARCTIC & ANTARCTIC

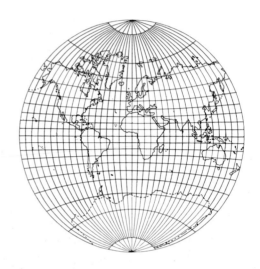

Life in the Arctic and Antarctic

The Arctic and Antarctic regions are at opposite sides of the world.

At the centre of the Arctic is the North Pole at the top of the world, while the South Pole is in the middle of the Antarctic at the bottom. The Arctic is a vast area of ice floating on the Arctic Ocean. The ice can be just a few metres thick in some areas and more than 30 metres in others. It can shift and break up, and when this happens the pieces of ice are known as *ice floes*.

The Antarctic is a frozen desert of ice, but the ice has frozen on land which means that the Antarctic is much colder than the Arctic because frozen earth is colder than the icy sea. The average thickness of the ice is 2000 metres; in parts it can be 4000 metres thick. There are theories that many thousands of years ago this land was much closer to the equator, with a warmer climate, so more living species could live there. Gradually the land drifted down to the far south to much colder temperatures — the average temperature is −25°C.

A cup of boiling water if thrown into the air of the Antarctic freezes instantly.

Arctic ice floes breaking up

Living things

Walruses, polar bears, whales and many different types of seal live in the Arctic. In summer, grasses and plants can grow and hundreds of insects live amongst the mosses and lichens.

But there are not only plants and animals living in the Arctic . . . the Inuit of North America and Greenland, the Lapp people of northern Europe and the Chukchi of north-eastern Siberia live there too.

Walrus

Mosses and lichens growing in summer

Inuit people

In the Antarctic there are many types of penguins and other seabirds such as albatrosses, shearwaters and skuas. They rely very much on eating a type of fish known as krill, which swim around in swarms in the ocean.

The only people who live in the Antarctic are the researchers who come from all over the world to carry out vital environmental and scientific studies. There are theories that the Antarctic is a region rich in oil and minerals.

Environmentalists are worried about the number of whales that have been killed by hunters over the years. Several species are in danger of becoming extinct and so there is a lot of support today throughout the world for those people who campaign for the protection of the whale. The World Wide Fund for Nature and Greenpeace are two organisations that believe in this.

Wandering Albatross chick on nest

Survival

The Arctic and Antarctic have attracted explorers for many years. They are motivated by the challenge of conquering the most inhospitable places in the world. Nowadays, equipment has become more sophisticated to cope with extremes in conditions and temperatures.

Food

Eating the right sort of food for the conditions is, of course, very important. Many foods can be processed to make them keep a long time, keep them light and make them easy to prepare. Here is a photograph of one man's rations on Captain Scott's expedition in 1912.

Food rations in 1912

Clothing suitable for Polar expeditions

Clothes

When temperatures are well below freezing point, keeping the body warm is crucial. Today people living in or exploring the Arctic and Antarctic follow the 'layer principle'. Several layers of lightweight rather than thick, heavy clothes are worn. In 1912 Captain Scott and four other British explorers set out to become the first men to reach the South Pole. They reached the Pole only to discover that a Norwegian explorer had got there before them. On the journey back to their home base the weather became very severe. It was bitterly cold, and they were sweating a lot because they had to drag their sledges with them. Their sweat froze and their clothes became wet, and they didn't have enough fuel to dry them out. Cold, damp and tired, they all died.

Wally Herbert and Ken Hedges
in their tent

Shelter

In the Antarctic, stations are set up for research groups. Often national governments assist these groups financially, which allows them to buy new equipment.

It is difficult when researchers or explorers are transporting their equipment and provisions. They put up tents or construct shelters as insulation against the cold nights.

Transport

Today machines like the sno-cat and the skidoo have become more reliable and are used by researchers to transport equipment.

Travelling by skidoo in the Antarctic

On top of the world

Wally Herbert is a British explorer who, in 1968, led a team of three men, four sledges and forty dogs from Alaska to Spitsbergen via the North Pole — it was the longest continuous sledge journey in the history of polar exploration. Wally learnt a lot from the Inuit about how to handle husky dogs. He decided to use huskies because he could not risk the possibility of a machine breaking down.

Dogs could also jump across cracks in the ice and swim if they fell in the sea. Wally also said that dogs could warn them of the approach of a bear, as polar bears can be extremely fierce.

Wally successfully completed his journey after fifteen months on the Arctic Ocean.

Husky dogs pulling a sledge

Words to travel with

Glossary

abhorrent *(p.52)*
  loathsome

amulet *(p.6)*
  a good-luck charm

banshee *(p.56)*
  a female ghost who, it
  was believed, gave out
  a mournful wail to
  announce a coming
  death

bole *(p.84)*
  trunk

benison *(p.53)*
  a blessing

cicadas *(p.4)*
  insects, a bit like
  grasshoppers

bestial *(p.83)*
  cruel, savage

Glossary continues
on page 112

convulsive (*p.58*)
  moving jerkily, violently

cyclamen (*p.9*)
  flower of the primrose family

decamp (*p.56*)
  go away, leave suddenly

facile (*p.54*)
  flexible

feint (*p.84*)
  to pretend an attack in one direction when really meaning another

ferocity (*p.83*)
  fierceness

fetish (*p.7*)
  an object believed to have magical powers

galvanising (*p.58*)
  exciting, startling

gnarled (*p.41*)
  covered with knots or lumps

harlequin (*p.58*)
  a character in a pantomime with patterned costume and a mask

heredity (*p.52*)
  qualities inherited from ancestors

ineffectual (*p.55*)
  not achieving the result that was intended

machete (*p.82*)
  a broad heavy knife

organdie (*p.4*)
  a fine transparent fabric of cotton or silk

pelts (*p.60*)
  skins of animals

perceive (*p.42*)
  make out

perplexity (*p.58*)
  confusion, feeling muddled

plaintive (*p.52*)
  sorrowful

primeval (*p.41*)
  of the earliest age

protruding (*p.44*)
  sticking out

relentless (*p.56*)
  never stopping

resignedly (*p.50*)
  giving in, not protesting any more

seer (*p.60*)
  someone who can see into the future

static (*p.19*)
  unwanted signals, interference

undaunted (*p.53*)
  not discouraged

unheeding (*p.53*)
  taking no notice of

sextant (*p.95*)
  an instrument to help find the way by measuring the positions of the stars

sonorous (*p.42*)
  pleasantly rich or loud

sporran (*p.95*)
  leather pouch covered in fur worn in front of the kilt with traditional Highland dress in Scotland